The food and cooking of
South China

Discover the vibrant tastes of Cantonese, Shantou, Hakka and Island cuisine

The food and cooking of
South China

traditions ★ tastes ★ techniques ★ 75 recipes ★ 400 photographs

Terry Tan

with photography by Martin Brigdale

This edition is published by Aquamarine, an imprint of Anness Publishing Ltd, Hermes House, 88–89 Blackfriars Road, London SE1 8HA tel. 020 7401 2077; fax 020 7633 9499

www.aquamarinebooks.com
www.annesspublishing.com

If you like the images in this book and would like to investigate using them for publishing, promotions or advertising, please visit our website www.practicalpictures.com for more information.

UK agent: The Manning Partnership Ltd; tel. 01225 478444; fax 01225 478440; sales@manning-partnership.co.uk

UK distributor: Grantham Book Services Ltd; tel. 01476 541080; fax 01476 541061; orders@gbs.tbs-ltd.co.uk

North American agent/distributor: National Book Network; tel. 301 459 3366; fax 301 429 5746; www.nbnbooks.com

Australian agent/distributor: Pan Macmillan Australia; tel. 1300 135 113; fax 1300 135 103; customer.service@macmillan.com.au

New Zealand agent/distributor: David Bateman Ltd; tel. (09) 415 7664; fax (09) 415 8892

Publisher: Joanna Lorenz
Senior Editor: Lucy Doncaster
Text Editors: Jenni Fleetwood and Catherine Best
Photography: Martin Brigdale
Food Stylist: Lucy McKelvie
Prop Stylist: Helen Trent
Designer: Simon Daley
Illustrator: Rob Highton
Production Controller: Wendy Lawson

© Anness Publishing Ltd 2008

Ethical Trading Policy

At Anness Publishing we believe that business should be conducted in an ethical and ecologically sustainable way, with respect for the environment and a proper regard to the replacement of the natural resources we employ.

As a publisher, we use a lot of wood pulp to make high-quality paper for printing, and that wood commonly comes from spruce trees. We are therefore currently growing more than 750,000 trees in three Scottish forest plantations: Berrymoss (130 hectares/ 320 acres), West Touxhill (125 hectares/ 305 acres) and Deveron Forest (75 hectares/ 185 acres). The forests we manage contain more than 3.5 times the number of trees employed each year in making paper for the books we manufacture.

Because of this ongoing ecological investment programme, you, as our customer, can have the pleasure and reassurance of knowing that a tree is being cultivated on your behalf to naturally replace the materials used to make the book you are holding.

Our forestry programme is run in accordance with the UK Woodland Assurance Scheme (UKWAS) and will be certified by the internationally recognized Forest Stewardship Council (FSC). The FSC is a non-government organization dedicated to promoting responsible management of the world's forests.

Certification ensures forests are managed in an environmentally sustainable and socially responsible way. For further information about this scheme, go to www.annesspublishing.com/trees

Notes

Bracketed terms are intended for American readers.

For all recipes, quantities are given in both metric and imperial measures and, where appropriate, in standard cups and spoons. Follow one set of measures, but not a mixture, because they are not interchangeable.

Standard spoon and cup measures are level. 1 tsp = 5ml, 1 tbsp = 15ml, 1 cup = 250ml/8fl oz.

Australian standard tablespoons are 20ml. Australian readers should use 3 tsp in place of 1 tbsp for measuring small quantities of gelatine, flour, salt, etc.

American pints are 16fl oz/2 cups. American readers should use 20fl oz/2.5 cups in place of 1 pint when measuring liquids.

Electric oven temperatures in this book are for conventional ovens. When using a fan oven, the temperature will probably need to be reduced by about 10–20°C/ 20–40°F. Since ovens vary, check with your manufacturer's instruction book for guidance.

The nutritional analysis given for each recipe is calculated per portion (i.e. serving or item), unless otherwise stated. If the recipe gives a range, such as Serves 4–6, then the nutritional analysis will be for the smaller portion size, i.e. 6 servings.

Measurements for sodium do not include salt added to taste.

Medium (US large) eggs are used unless otherwise stated in the text.

The very young, the elderly, pregnant women and those in ill-health or with a compromised immune system are advised against consuming dishes containing raw eggs, meat or fish.

Front cover shows Pork and Prawn Dumplings – for recipe, see page 54.

Contents

Geography and climate

From the bustling market stalls of high-rise Hong Kong to rural kitchens in the outlying villages of the province, the people of southern China share a passion for their food. Differentiated from the rest of the country by its maritime climate and close trading links with the outside world, the area is divided into four smaller gastronomic subdivisions: Hainan Island, Hong Kong, Guangdong, and Shantou, a town within Guangdong Province. Each of these has its own signature dishes, which reflect the cooking techniques and ingredients particular to that place.

A land of waterways, the south of China comprises the province of Guangdong, Hainan Island and Hong Kong. It is trisected by three rivers, the Xi Jiang (West River), Bei Jiang (North River) and Dong Jiang (East River). Their confluence forms the Zhu Jiang (Pearl River) and its delta runs into the South China Sea.

With such ready access to fresh water and the sea, it is perhaps little surprise that local dishes often feature seafood, whether as the star turn or as an additional flavour. From prawns (shrimp) and lobster to carp and snapper, everything is used to create a wide and delectable range of regional culinary treats.

The terrain surrounding the rivers and coast varies: the north of Guangdong province is quite mountainous, while in the south the land tends to be lower and flatter, with fertile delta wetlands. These lower-lying parts are ideal for growing crops, especially rice, and for raising livestock like poultry and pigs, making the region fairly self-sufficient. Isolated from the rest of the country by the mountains, locals have an outward-looking attitude, and are receptive to new ideas.

Left With a moist, warm climate and access to many waterways, south China produces a wide range of food products. *Below* The third largest country in the world, China has a land area of about 3.7 million sq miles/9.6 million sq km.

A warm, wet climate

The yearly average temperature in the south of the country is a tolerable 26°C/79°F, but this does not reflect the heat and humidity of the long summer, which can stretch from April to October. There are also frequent typhoons ('great wind' in Cantonese) between May and November, which can lash the region with great ferocity, disrupting transport and other local amenities. With frequent precipitation and long hours of sunshine, however, the region has ideal year-round growing conditions.

The delta wetlands and the low-lying Luizhou coastal plain, including Hainan Island, are especially fertile and support abundant rice crops as well as other staple foods like corn and peanuts. The sub-tropical climate, regular rainfall and sunshine found here also allow crops like tea, tobacco, sugar cane, bananas, pineapples, oranges, tangerines, longans and lychees to grow in profusion. Some of these fruits are incorporated into local dishes, adding a sweet note.

Hainan Island is the only truly tropical region in China, and produces crops such as coffee and rubber. Scorching hot for most of the year, the months from late January to March offer the most comfortable temperatures, and the clement winter months are nowhere near as harsh as those in the north.

Local tribes

Famous for its magnificent local Cantonese cuisine, south China has always attracted migrants from both abroad and other regions of the country. Some indigenous tribes have survived, though, and there are thought to be about 39 minority tribes. Of these, the Li are the most numerous, with more than one million people. Believed to have migrated to the area from Fujian some 3,000 years ago, this hardy race have for centuries struggled to scratch a subsistence. Their livelihood today, however, depends largely on tourism and hospitality.

Contact with other cultures over the centuries has resulted in the introduction of new ingredients and cooking techniques to the local pool of culinary knowledge. This is particularly evident in Macau, where many Portuguese influences, including Egg Tarts, can be seen on the menu, and in Hong Kong, famous for its culinary innovation.

Hainan Island

Formerly administered as part of Guangdong, Hainan Island is now a separate province. Blessed with superb beaches on the southern coast, the island has wild, thickly forested mountains at its heart, and its small villages are peopled by hill tribes.

Above left The tropical climate of the delta wetlands produces abundant rice crops. Above Hong Kong is as famous for its cuisine as for its skyline.

Lying on the same latitude as Hawaii and Hanoi in Vietnam, the region is often called China's Hawaii and is an irresistible winter holiday destination for mainlanders from the north and west seeking to escape the bitter cold of their home provinces. Tourism is, therefore, big business, and many hedonistic resorts have sprung up on the south coast, creating a Chinese Costa del Sol.

Hong Kong

The bustling island of Hong Kong is often considered to be something of a maverick, both because it was a Sino-British colony until its handover to China in 1997 and because it has always had an independent soul that is receptive to external influences.

The 426sq mile/1,103sq km territory is divided into four main areas: Hong Kong Island, Kowloon, the New Territories and the relatively under-populated Outlying Islands. In gourmet terms, Hong Kong Island and Kowloon have been the most influential as their forward-thinking people are cut from a feisty fabric, ever inventive in their culinary endeavours, which are recognized the world over.

History and migration

The region that now comprises southern China was for many years relatively untouched by the activities of more northern peoples, and it wasn't until the 6th century that Guangdong officially became part of China. Populated by indigenous tribes, the rural region slowly changed as people migrated further north, and traders from abroad introduced both new ingredients and the new religion of Islam. Subsequent changes occurred as large numbers of intrepid Cantonese people emigrated overseas, while Portuguese and British traders arrived to capitalize on the rich trading potential at the bustling ports.

With easy access to the South China Sea, the southern provinces have always been a lure for foreigners, and it is thought that the region was visited by outsiders as early as the 2nd century AD, when the Romans briefly passed by.

The development of south China

In the early first centuries AD, when the rest of China was busy carving out a civilization on the Yangtze River, south China was very much a rural backwater peopled by native tribes, the last survivors of which form the minority groups scattered throughout the region today.

Although Chinese administration in the region began with the Qin Dynasty (221–206BC), which established the first unified Chinese empire, it was not until the era of the Three Kingdoms in the late 3rd century AD that Guangdong earned its provincial status as part of China.

From 221BC until the end of the 3rd century, the demographics of what is now Guangdong slowly shifted, and there were several periods of nomadic immigration from the north of China, particularly at times of political turmoil. In addition, traders from as far afield as the Middle East arrived in the region in the 7th century, lured by the promise of silk, exquisite porcelain and tea, and leaving in their wake the heritage of Islam as well as an awareness of new ingredients.

Around this time, the province of Guangdong enjoyed a degree of autonomy. The Tang Dynasty (AD618–907) was one of the most progressive periods in Chinese history and the imperial leaders set up a special residential quarter south of the Pearl River especially for foreigners who chose to stay in China for reasons of trade. As a result, Guangzhou became a rich and prosperous port, frequented by Arab, Persian, Malaysian and Western merchants, making the fertile region even more attractive to Chinese people from the north, who flocked to the area in droves, hoping to make their fortunes.

China meets the world

In addition to moving around within China, the Cantonese had a tendency to look beyond the boundaries of their own country and venture further afield. This intrepid spirit was encouraged by early Ming emperors, and resulted in a number of renowned explorers, the most famous of whom was Admiral Cheng Ho, a Muslim

Left **This painting at a temple shrine in Penang, Malaysia, depicts Admiral Cheng Ho (1371–1433).**

eunuch who was the first Chinese person to set foot in Malacca, off the west coast of Malaysia, between 1409 and 1411.

This contact with the outside world was further enhanced by the arrival of European settlers, the Portuguese, in 1557. They established the first European settlement in the country in Macau, on the southern coast of Guangdong, where they had a great degree of autonomy, administering the region until the hand-over in 1997.

The British arrived in the 17th century and by the early 1700s Guangzhou, already a busy trading port, had become even more wealthy. This was helped in no small part by an imperial edict that created a merchant's guild, giving the port a monopoly on China's trade with foreign countries. The province of Guangdong as a whole benefited and, with easy access to the outer world, it became a staging post for emigrants leaving the increasingly overpopulated region to seek work abroad.

Right *A junk in full sail heads toward the skyscrapers of the Wan Chai district of Hong Kong.*

In 1842, the British influence strengthened even further when Hong Kong was ceded to them. Although it was originally thought of as a far-flung Chinese outpost, by the middle of the 20th century it had developed into a buzzing trading and financial centre with an exceedingly vibrant social climate. Despite fears about what would happen after the 1997 handover, Hong Kong still retains a free-market economy and its own legal and social system. Mainland political observers describe the current situation as 'One country, two systems'.

The Cantonese abroad

Although people had been leaving the southern region for centuries, it wasn't until the early 19th century that the first large-scale instance of emigration occurred. At this time, many people of Cantonese, Hakka or Fujian stock left China to seek their fortunes in such far-flung places as South-east Asia, Britain, Australia, Canada, the United States and the Philippines. They took with them their culinary knowledge, and successfully established the innumerable Cantonese restaurants and Chinese food stores that can be found in towns and cities all over the world today.

Regional cooking

When considering Chinese regional cooking styles, one must bear in mind the fact that despite the vastness of the country and the diversity of climates and resources, many dishes are eaten everywhere in the country, with only slight regional takes on countrywide classics. Having said this, the food of southern China is notable for the abundance of seafood on the menu and for its simple preparation, allowing natural flavours and textures to carry the dish. Dim sum also plays a crucial role, and this tradition of eating many small morsels, now so popular elsewhere in China and, indeed, the rest of the world, originated in Guangdong in the 10th century.

Across the regions, daily meals are prepared on the ancient premise of *fan-cai* principles. This is literally translated as 'rice and dishes'. Put simply, it means the combination of the staple dishes of rice, grains and various forms of dumplings (*fan*) and a variety of cooked vegetables, meat or seafood (*cai*). The ultimate objective is a perfect synergy between the two basic ingredients, plus a harmonious balance of the four fundamental elements of colour, aroma, flavour and shape. This is a tenet that applies to every individual dish as well as to the whole meal.

Centuries of exposure to foreign elements have enriched Cantonese cuisine hugely, and adventurous chefs have refined and developed their remarkable styles of cooking throughout the world, wherever they have settled.

Taste and texture
The key feature of Cantonese food and cooking is an emphasis on different textures. Natural flavours are not altered and preparation is kept to a minimum; what is aimed for is the control of crispness and smoothness, leading to a subtle and complex overall texture.

One example of how this quest for texture is manifested is barbecue or 'hung' roasting. This highly developed art involves parboiling the meat to melt some of the fat, inflating the meat with air and hanging up to dry, which promotes a crispy skin, and finally slathering with a sweet glaze and roasting to produce a glossy, crunchy finish.

After texture, the second most distinctive aspect of the cuisine is its savoury quality, and how flavours are combined to maximize this preference. Seafood, for instance, is mixed with meat in many dishes, in its natural form or as sauces. Salted black beans are also used to impart a savoury taste, while shredded ginger or chopped coriander (cilantro) are used to counteract any overpowering fishiness.

Below left Rice is served with a range of dishes in accordance with fan cai *principles. Below 'Hung' roasting is a popular way of preparing many types of meat.*

Soy sauces are often used in artful ways to bring out the flavours of meat and poultry, married with aromatics such as leeks, ginger and onions. Fruit is likewise often incorporated in Cantonese cooking, and citrus fruits like lemons, plums, tangerines and oranges are key ingredients in the tangy, sweet and sour sauces.

Three regional styles

As a result of centuries of immigration, the province of Guangzhou features many sub-dialects within its borders. This diversity is reflected in Cantonese cuisine, which embraces three distinct schools, each based around its own individual dialect group: Canton; Swatow (Chaozhou) from the city of Shandou; and the Hakkas from the region known as Dong Jiang.

The Canton school fields by far the largest spread of dishes; some, like stinky tofu, an odorous delicacy from Hong Kong in which tofu is marinated in fermented vegetables for several months, so exotic that they have earned the cuisine its great reputation for adventurousness. Swatow or Shandou cuisine, on the other hand, is notable for its clear flavours and seafood dishes.

Hakka or Dong Jiang food is somewhat different; it has a distinct regional character, with many more rustic dishes that reflect the peasant culture. There is a trend toward thrift among Hakka cooks, who are loath to waste anything, from the tiniest bits of meat to any offcuts of ingredients they can get. As a result of this parsimonious approach, Hakka cuisine resembles more closely the food of the neighbouring province of Fujian, with its simpler culinary traditions. Unlike many others in south China, Hakka people eat beef, since they do not regard the cow as a sacred animal.

One factor that links all three schools is the close relationship between the food and eating habits and the history and culture of the region. For instance, cooks love wrapping food in leaves, as in Glutinous Rice in a Lotus Leaf, because this style of cooking reflects the largely pastoral nature of the area – a connection that is treasured even today.

Hong Kong and Macau

Universally recognized as the supreme pinnacle of Cantonese cuisine, the food of Hong Kong is renowned throughout the country and the world. Its style is

Above left Restaurants in Hong Kong, like this floating one, are notable for the innovative nature of the food they serve. Above The famous egg tarts made in Macau are Portuguese in origin, reflecting the town's heritage.

related both to ancient classical tradition and to contemporary mores. Classic dishes have evolved over time as a result of the island's long exposure to foreign cooking methods and ingredients, as well as being driven by high levels of competition and innovation in restaurant kitchens. On a cosmopolitan island populated by wealthy business people, this cutting edge is essential if an eatery is to survive. In a bid to attract customers, many Chinese restaurants take pride in promoting dishes as being 'Hong Kong style', which really means 'Cantonese with attitude'.

The town of Macau is a former Portuguese colony that follows the same inventive approach as Hong Kong when it comes to cooking. Hence, Lobster Noodles, Portuguese Egg Tarts and other fusion dishes are typical of the menus in this area, making them stand out from the dishes that are eaten elsewhere in the south.

Festivals and celebrations

In the whole of China, the western or Gregorian calendar is followed for all practical purposes, but it is the lunar calendar that governs the cultural, festive, religious and spiritual life of the people. Most of the major celebrations, such as the Lunar New Year, Moon Cake Festival and Dumpling Festival, have evolved over thousands of years and are important annual events everywhere.

Although many festivals are celebrated throughout the country, there are some major regional differences in how they are marked. These lie in the preparation of food as offerings and for family meals, with each regional variation reflecting indigenous ingredients and local customs. There are also different, smaller festivals tied to local history and traditions.

Whatever the occasion, Cantonese people pull out all the stops when it comes to preparing food. Edible treats form the delicious basis of every celebration, and what is going to be eaten is the topic of constant conversation in every Cantonese community in the lead-up to the event, from Shantou to Sydney and from Hong Kong to Hungary.

Lunar New Year

Falling on the first day of the first lunar month in the Chinese calendar (between 20 January and 21 February), Lunar New Year or Chinese New Year is a major holiday for Chinese people everywhere.

In the lead-up to the new year, homes are given a good clean and new clothes and hairstyles are worn, symbolizing renewal. On the eve of the event, there is usually a special family meal featuring a fish dish and, in the south, a special cake called *niangao* is made and pieces distributed to relatives and friends.

The day itself is marked with communal feasts and visits to family elders, as well as street parties and firework displays. Red, the colour of luck, can be seen everywhere, from decorations and the costumes worn by people in parades, to the red packet containing money that unmarried people receive.

Food containing symbolic ingredients plays an important role throughout the holiday, and there are various regional specialities, including the Cantonese chicken soup called 'broth of prosperity'. This contains shredded hen's eggs and pigeon or quail eggs, symbolizing gold and silver ingots, while the chicken symbolizes the phoenix rising from the ashes, meaning rebirth and rejuvenation.

Another favourite dish is braised, seasoned pork shoulder, which goes by the delightful name 'mist of harmony'. Almost all the major ingredients are imbued with meaning: transparent vermicelli (*fun si*) are referred to as 'silvery threads of longevity'; platters of chicken wings represent 'soaring one thousand miles'; and bamboo shoots are eaten because they grow so tall, meaning 'year after year, ascend to great heights'.

Flowers and fruits also play significant roles. Lotus blossoms are the symbol of womanhood, and the Goddess of Mercy (Kuan Yin), patron of seafarers, is always portrayed standing on a lotus

Far left Red, the colour of good luck, can be seen everywhere during the Lunar New Year, including street parades. *Left* Moon cakes can be stuffed with various fillings, including meat, pastes and eggs, as here.

Above **The annual dragon boat race is part of a colourful and highly competitive event enjoyed by everyone.**

leaf and carrying a lotus stem. Oranges and kumquats are a symbolic gift and during the New Year Cantonese people will never visit anyone without a pair of these fruits. Pomegranates, studded with jewel-like seeds, are also important as they symbolize fertility and good fortune.

Tin Hau or T'ien Hou

This Hong Kong festival on the 23rd day of the third lunar month (late April/early May) is in homage to Tin Hau, the Goddess of the Sky, who is said to safeguard fishermen against storms and keep them from drowning. In southern coastal regions dominated by fishing communities there are numerous holy shrines constructed in her honour. The festival itself is also known as the Festival of Bun Hills in the south of China, after the spectacular bun towers that are created – large bamboo structures several storeys high heaped with special sweet buns that are reputed to bring good luck. People climb up the towers, picking up as many buns as they can possibly hold.

In addition to the bun towers there are magnificent processions and parades, with people dressed in costumes reflecting the imperial past, riding on flowered floats and walking on stilts. The young play a major role in the processions, with children perched above the crowd on vertiginous stilts. There is food of all kinds to be had, although the collecting and eating of sweet buns is the main focus.

Dumpling or Dragon Boat Festival

This is celebrated on the fifth day of the fifth lunar month (June/July) and is marked with the eating of rice and meat dumplings. The 'dragon boat' refers to the time when a court official, Qu Yuan, was drowned in a river. In an attempt to rescue him, his comrades are said to have rowed up and down the river looking for him. This incident has since mutated into a colourful festival with teams of rowers competing in races (to represent the quest to find Qu Yuan), many of their boats decorated with a heraldic symbol of a dragon or a phoenix to boost their competitive spirit.

Right **Children are dressed in special costumes and hoisted aloft as part of the Tin Hau Festival in Hong Kong.**

Moon Cake Festival

Also known as the Mid-Autumn Festival, this celebration occurs on the 15th day of the 8th lunar month (September/October). The most significant culinary element is the appearance of moon cakes, round pastries that represent the shape of the full moon, stuffed with all manner of fillings, like meat, almond paste and salted duck's eggs.

Sending the Kitchen God to heaven

Taoism is practised devoutly in the south of China, and the people pay reverent homage to its pantheon of gods and goddesses all over Guangzhou, especially in Hong Kong.

One of the most important dates is the 24th day of the 11th month (December/January), when the Kitchen God takes his leave of Earth and ascends to his celestial home. Of all the Taoist deities, he is the most identified with the household and all that it represents – from food to birth and death – and according to tradition paper effigies of him should be smeared with honey so he will only have good things to report to his celestial elders.

Cooking tools and equipment

The traditional southern Chinese kitchen is quite basic, often simply consisting of an open hearth and simple implements such as woks, cleavers and rustic pots. Convection ovens are not often used in Chinese kitchens, and most cooking takes place on top of a fire or a hob. Preparation of ingredients is generally kept to a minimum, so only a small selection of knives and other implements are required.

In addition to frying food in the invaluable wok, which appears in every southern Chinese kitchen, cooks also steam ingredients with a range of aromatics in bamboo steamers, positioned above simmering water in a wok, or in stand-alone steamboats. Special rice cookers, imported from Japan, are also common in modern kitchens.

Athough not suitable for baking, clay or sand pots make useful serving vessels, and ensure that food is served sizzling hot. Chopsticks are used during cooking as well as for eating the food, and are a handy and safe alternative to tongs for turning a piece of food while it is frying.

Below Traditional kitchens comprise only basic implements, such as woks and clay serving vessels.

Woks and ladles

Quite the most important utensil in every Chinese kitchen, the wok dates back centuries to the early period of nomadic tribes in north China. Because these people were always on the move, they needed a utensil that could sit on a few rocks over a makeshift fire. This pan had to have a round bottom so that it would not wobble. The wok was born and has never changed its basic shape since then, varying only in size. Today, as then, it performs multiple functions in Chinese households as a steamer, a braising pan, a frying pan and even a shallow boiler.

The best woks are made of heavy cast iron. Non-stick woks are not ideal for rapid stir-frying as the action may chip the Teflon coating. Stainless steel is not the best material either, as it conducts heat too rapidly and may burn food. Electric woks are a recent innovation but are also not perfect, as the heat is not sufficiently high for quick stir-frying. They are good for slow braising and steaming, however. Cast iron – an alloy of iron and carbon – is still considered the best material for woks, although cast aluminium, being much lighter and less expensive, is increasingly used.

The traditional wok ladle is shaped at an angle that matches the curvature of the wok. This enables better scooping and more efficient stir-frying, as the blade has a broader area than a wooden spoon and other conventional ladles.

Below Bamboo steamers are ideal vessels for gently cooking food above a wok of simmering water.

Above A modern metal cleaver is ideal for chopping most ingredients, from meat to aromatics and vegetables.

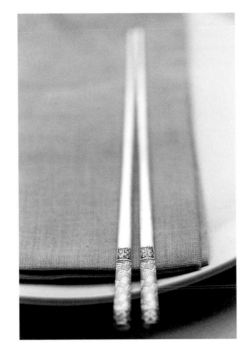

Above Silver chopsticks were used in imperial times as a way of avoiding poisoning, and are still used today.

Cleaver

A unique Chinese knife made of tempered iron or steel, honed to razor sharpness, the best size for a cleaver is about 30cm/12in in length and 10cm/4in wide, with a wooden handle. These days, however, they are mostly made of one complete piece of metal. The cleaver provides essential leverage for cutting through bone and large pieces of meat, and is a versatile implement – it can be used as a carver, crusher, slicer and chopper. The blunt end serves as a makeshift mallet for tenderizing meats.

Clay or sand pot

This Chinese dish comes with a single handle and serves as an oven-to-table utensil when food needs to be served piping hot or sizzling. Traditional clay pots have a wire frame to support the structure as the intense heat can cause cracks. This kind of pot is never used for the whole cooking process. Dishes are cooked in a wok or other heatproof vessel and then transferred to the clay pot, which is pre-heated just enough to maintain the temperature at the table.

Steamer

Traditionally made of woven bamboo, steamers come in many sizes – small enough to contain bitesize morsels or large enough to contain several chickens. Bamboo is best as the lids are porous and do not trap the steam inside, which can result in water-logged food, although these days they may also be made of aluminium, with multiple perforated trays to allow the steam to come through each layer. Multiple stack steamers are ideal for cooking several dishes at the same time.

Steamboat

Originating in Mongolia, steamboats are sometimes called fire pots or hot pots, and are usually made of brass-coated or enamel-coated metal with a funnel in the centre of a moat. Stock or water is poured into this moat and the whole dish used to be heated with charcoal, although it is more common these days to see electric models with thermostatic controls. Various foods are cut up and placed around the steamboat so that diners can cook the food themselves, using brass wire spoons.

Bamboo draining basket

Ubiquitous in all Asian countries, this versatile utensil is used for many purposes – as a strainer, for draining soaked rice, or even as a food cover that allows air to circulate while keeping out flying insects.

Chopsticks

For many centuries, the Chinese have preferred bamboo chopsticks for their slightly rough texture, which is best for taking up slippery foods like noodles and sauce-based dishes. Imperial households, however, tended to use ivory and silver ones. Those made with silver were adopted to detect any poisons, as silver reacts to any toxic element. Given the amount of intrigue in the dynastic courts, they were life-savers. Normal chopsticks are 22cm/9in long, but longer ones – up to twice this length – are used for turning deep-fried foods, keeping the user at a safe distance from spitting hot oil.

Rice cookers

Having always been used in Chinese and Asian homes, rice cookers are now appearing in more western kitchens, as restaurants make use of this marvellous Japanese invention. Electric models now also have features for keeping rice warm for up to an hour. These work on the principle of weight – when all the liquid evaporates, the inner container, which sits on a spring-loaded element, rises automatically, switching the appliance off.

Classic ingredients

From bland staples like rice and all types of noodle, to piquant and aromatic sauces and crisp, fresh vegetables, southern Chinese cooks make good use of a wide range of ingredients. Carefully prepared with minimal fuss, these are then transformed into a wealth of mouthwatering dishes, many of which are served at once as part of a communal meal in carefully thought-out combinations that adhere to the principles of fan cai.

The cuisine of south China uses many different ingredients in incredibly inventive ways. Each dish is cooked and presented with great care and attention to detail, particularly in the blending of tastes, textures and colours.

Noodles

While rice remains the staple starch of any Chinese meal, noodles are ideal when time is short as they make a complete meal in one dish, simply stir-fried or more elaborately combined with meat, fish and vegetables.

Fine rice noodles There are several dried types of fine noodle, including rice vermicelli, or *mi fun*. They are usually used in soup dishes.

Fresh rice noodles The Cantonese stir up an iconic dish with fresh rice noodles

Below, left to right **Cooked long grain rice, mung bean noodles, rice flour and rice noodles.**

called *hor fun*, rich with beef, seafood or pork and vegetables.

Mung bean noodles These are also known as cellophane or glass noodles and are made from mung bean flour. They are sold dried, but reconstitute rapidly when soaked in warm water, and keep their crunch.

Wheat flour noodles These noodles come either dried, to be reconstituted, or fresh, to be blanched before use in stir-fries or soup.

Rice

No southern Chinese would dream of sitting down to a meal, however simple, without a bowl of rice. There are two basic methods of cooking rice – boiling or steaming – and when cooked and cooled, it forms the basis of fried rice.

Glutinous rice Both long grain and short grain glutinous rice have to be soaked for several hours before they yield their fluffiness or succulence. Although the

texture of cooked glutinous rice is quite firm, it is nevertheless sticky and it is this that makes it popular as a wraparound for a range of filled rice dishes.

Ground rice or rice flour This is used in making all kinds of sticky cakes, dumplings and pancakes, and as a thickener for soups and stews.

Rice papers These delicate triangular or circular papers make delicate spring rolls or wrappers for deep-fried seafood.

Spices and other flavourings

Many flavourings are used in southern Chinese cooking, either on their own or in combination, and the savoury, spicy or sweet notes add a tang to dishes.

Black bean and yellow bean paste Soy beans are roasted and fermented with salt, then used whole or ground into a thick paste.

Chillies Fresh chillies are chopped finely and added to many stir-fries, lending the dish a fiery kick and a dash of colour.

Chilli bean paste This is a fiery purée of ground dried chillies blended with yellow bean paste.

Dried fish Fundamental in Cantonese cooking, small dried fish are usually deep-fried and used to make delicious crunchy side dishes or a garnish for stir-fried vegetables.

Five-spice powder Indispensable in Cantonese stews and as a spice for spring roll fillings, this is a blend of powdered aniseed, fennel, cloves, cinnamon and pepper.

Garlic This aromatic bulb is used in a number of stir-fried dishes, filling the kitchen with its distinctive aroma.

Ginger The tender stems of root ginger are ground, chopped or puréed. They are integral to stir-fries and many dips.

Hoisin sauce This is a dark sauce made from a blend of yellow bean paste and sugar. It has a natural affinity with crispy aromatic duck pancakes or as a seasoning for stews and roast pork.

Sesame oil Widely used, this oil has an intense nutty fragrance that can overpower other seasonings, so a teaspoon or two is sufficient.

Soy sauce The underscoring element in Cantonese cuisine is soy sauce, which has been made for thousands of years. It is available in many varieties, and with additional flavourings, including chillies. It is to the East what salt is to the West.

Above, left to right Garlic, red chillies, soy sauce, hoisin sauce.

Stock Making your own stock only requires the simplest ingredients. The Chinese traditionally use meat and poultry stocks in many recipes, but the recipe for vegetable stock given here is a flavourful substitute. It will keep well for up to a week or more when refrigerated. It can also be frozen for up to three months. Freeze it in ice cube trays for when you need small amounts for stir-fried dishes. One cube yields about 15ml/1 tbsp.

Vinegar Black and red rice vinegars are used as the basic souring agent in most soups and as dips for dumplings and fried foods.

Meat, poultry and eggs

Although southern dishes do feature other meats, pork and poultry are the mainstays that form the basis of many savoury recipes.

Beef Expensive and hard to come by, beef is mainly eaten on special occasions, especially by Hakka people who do not venerate the cow as a sacred animal, unlike many other Chinese people.

Chicken This is probably the most widely eaten food in China. There are many favourite dishes, including a brew made from chicken and ginseng that is is believed to improve the memory.

Vegetable stock

Makes 1 litre/1¾ pints/4 cups

45ml/3 tbsp peanut oil
4 large carrots, sliced
4 large celery stalks with
  leaves, sliced
3 large onions, coarsely chopped
5ml/1 tsp salt
10 white peppercorns
1.5 litres/2½ pints/6¼ cups
  cold water

1 Heat the peanut oil in a large pan. When it is almost smoking, add the carrots, celery and onions.

2 Reduce the heat to medium and cook until the vegetables are soft but not browned, stirring occasionally, about 2–3 minutes.

3 Add the seasonings and water and increase the heat to bring to a vigorous boil. Cover the pan, reduce heat to simmer, and cook for 1 hour.

4 Strain the stock through a fine sieve (strainer) and press down to extract every bit of juice. Refrigerate for up to a week in a sealed container or pour into an ice cube tray and freeze.

Duck Soy-braised Duck is just one of the many traditional southern dishes, and classic Peking duck and crispy aromatic duck have become premium dishes in Cantonese restaurants all over the world.

Eggs In addition to hen's eggs, which are used in many dishes, duck's eggs and quail's eggs are also enjoyed. Duck's eggs are usually available salted or as century eggs – eggs that are coated with a paste made of mud and rice husks and kept in a dark place for weeks until their whites turn black and their yolks a dull grey. Quail's eggs are sold widely and usually end up in soups. Hard-boiled eggs of all types are often served to elders on their birthdays as symbols of completeness and respect. These are usually cooked with noodles in a sugary broth as the sweetness also denotes a good life ahead.

Offal (variety meats) Chinese cooks have elevated the art of cooking offal to great heights. Lungs with shredded bamboo shoots, liver with wine and garlic, kidney in soup redolent with ginger, trotters braised in soy sauce – these great dishes take pride of place in every Chinese home.

Pork Every bit of the pig is used in Cantonese cooking. Roast pork is made from a rib cut that is streaked with fat and cut as a long strip. For slow-cooking or braising, the leg cut is usually used. Suckling pig is a festive delicacy and no wedding banquet is considered complete without this scrumptious centrepiece. Lesser cuts are used for minced (ground) pork, the mainstay of dim sum fillings, and pork fat is rendered down to lard, in which many stir-fried dishes are cooked, giving them a distinct flavour.

Fish and shellfish

In every city, town and village in south China, there are wet markets where fishmongers sell absolutely fresh fish of a bewildering variety. Fish is cooked as soon as possible after being caught, and any leftovers are processed into cakes or balls, steamed or fried as savoury complements to a whole range of noodle and rice dishes.

Anchovies One of China's favourite foods, anchovies are best known in their dried form, and are also used extensively as a seasoning agent, especially in soup.

Crabs There are several varieties of crab available, the most common being 'mottled' or 'flower' crabs. These are cooked and flaked to be added to stir-fries or as a rich filling for dumplings.

Eels Plump adult eels are highly prized in stewed dishes containing lots of wine and ginger.

Mussels These flavoursome crustaceans are simply steamed or cooked in Chinese wine with garlic and ginger.

Prawns Both marine and freshwater prawns (shrimp) are highly prized by the Chinese. Juicy and meaty, the bigger ones

Above, left to right **Hen's eggs, chicken legs and wings, dried anchovies, raw prawns.**

are often grilled (broiled) whole, or added to stir-fries and curries; the small ones are dried and added to stocks to enhance the flavour.

Red snappers These distinctive fish are brightly coloured, with a delicate flavour and soft flesh, and are often simply steamed with a few aromatics.

Preparing crab

1 Make sure the crab is dry, with no sign of water in the shell. The shell should be firm and contain no cracks.

2 Turn the crab belly up and remove the soft V-shaped flap on the belly. Pull the top shell off the body.

3 Scoop out the soft, yellowish coral and reserve. Discard the feathery gills and snap off the legs and claws.

4 The larger claws should be cracked, but not entirely broken up, so the flesh can be easily extracted when cooked. Rinse the body and cut into two or more pieces.

Preparing fish

These general methods can be applied to most types of fish.

Scaling

1 Holding the fish firmly by the tail, use a round-bladed knife to scrape against the scales from tail to head.

Gutting

1 Holding the fish firmly, make a slit down the belly and remove all entrails. Use plastic gloves for this rather messy job as the fishy smell can linger.

2 With a pair of scissors, snip the gills to separate them, then remove.

3 Trim away all fins close to the body. Wash the fish and pat it dry.

Filleting

1 Holding the trimmed fish firmly against a chopping board, begin to slice from the tail end towards you. Cut as close as possible to the central bone and cut away two clean fillets.

2 Keep or freeze all the trimmings, as they make excellent fish stock.

Scallops These tasty morsels are often served steamed with ginger and garlic as an elegant Cantonese appetizer.

Snakeheads These eel-like fish are enjoyed for their meaty flesh and rich flavour and often feature in a soup dish made with fish and rice vermicelli.

Squid An important and plentiful seafood, squid can be cooked in a variety of ways, including quickly stir-fried or simmered in soup.

Vegetables

The most fundamental ingredients throughout China, vegetables are an intrinsic part of every Chinese meal.

Aubergines (eggplants) The common aubergine is long and thin, in shades of pale green or purple. It is incredibly versatile, served steamed, fried or stuffed.

Beansprouts These can be eaten raw but are usually stir-fried with noodles.

Bamboo shoots Bamboo enjoys a revered status within Chinese culture. The shoots are crunchy, with a distinctive, slightly astringent taste.

Chinese leaves Chinese leaves have a delicate, sweet aroma and are used in stir-fries, stews, soups or raw in salads.

Coriander (cilantro) This is indispensable as a garnish in soups and stews or chopped and mixed with spring roll fillings.

Daikon (mooli) This root vegetable looks like a large white carrot. It is crisp, juicy and slightly spicy in flavour. It can be eaten raw or cooked and is often grated and made into a dim sum savoury cake.

Dried and preserved vegetables At times of bumper harvests in south China, many vegetables are dried or salted for cooking in the winter months when fresh food is scarce. Mixed vegetables can also be pickled and kept for many months, adding their spicy, rich flavour to winter dishes or appearing as a tasty garnish.

Gourds and squashes Many different types of gourd and squash are eaten, including luffa squash, 'fuzzy' or 'hairy' melon and winter melon. They are best steamed or cooked in stews and soups.

Leeks There is a special place in Chinese cooking for leeks, which are often regarded as a good alternative to garlic, being aromatic and very versatile.

Mangetouts (snow peas) Crisp and tasty, these are one of the most common Chinese vegetables, with a range of uses. They make good fillings for spring rolls.

Mushrooms These are ubiquitous in southern Chinese cooking. Many varieties are used, including shiitake, cloud ear (wood ear), enoki, oyster, silver ear and straw mushrooms. They are often dried and then reconstituted in water before being added to stews, soups and stir-fries.

Below, left to right **Red snapper, raw squid, bamboo shoots, gai choy.**

Mustard greens These are large, pale green leaves known as *gai choy* in Cantonese. They have a sharp and robust flavour, and make a classic dish when poached with egg white and crab meat.

Pak choi (bok choy) Usually about 13cm/5in long with pale green stalks and dark, thin leaves, it makes excellent stir-fries.

Spring onions (scallions) In China these crunchy, mild onions are liberally used as a garnish, in many poultry and meat dishes, and are a fundamental part of most savoury dumpling recipes.

Tubers and aquatic roots and seeds These unusual vegetables include sweet cassava, bitter gingko nuts, fragrant lotus roots and seeds, creamy taro (yam) and crunchy water chestnuts. They are a speciality of Chinese cuisine and impart a distinctive flavour and texture to many dishes, especially sweet puddings.

Tofu

An ancient food that has been a Chinese mainstay for centuries, tofu or soy bean curd is much valued for its nutritional properties. It is protein- and iron-rich and low in calories, and has a neutral taste that is a perfect foil for absorbing other, stronger flavours.

Dried tofu Sold in long sticks, this is often found in nourishing Cantonese soups, both sweet and savoury.

Fermented tofu This is a favourite condiment, which is traditionally used in marinating poultry and as a rich seasoning for braised dishes.

Fresh tofu There are two main types of fresh tofu: soft and firm. The soft, 'silken' variety is best used in soups and steamed dishes, whereas the slightly rubbery firm variety works well in stir-fries.

Pressed tofu Cubes of fresh tofu are dried and pressed until they become firm cakes with a brown skin. These are then sliced and added to stir-fries.

Tofu skins These processed brown, wrinkly sheets are often used as spring roll and dim sum wrappers.

Tofu wafers These are light-brown pieces of slightly sweetened, dried tofu that can be fried as a garnish for stir-fried noodles or added to vegetable stews.

Fruit

Many exotic fruits grown in the tropical climate of south China are eaten as snacks or palate cleansers, especially following savoury dishes.

Bananas These are usually eaten fresh or fried. A number of savoury dishes include the blossoms of the banana plant.

Coconuts Ripe fruits are squeezed for a rich white milk that is essential in Chinese desserts and cakes, and is also used as a marinade for meat.

Jackfruits The texture of jackfruit is delightfully crunchy. It tastes rather like ripe mango, and the flesh is both creamy and chewy.

Limes These are used fresh or preserved in salt, as a snack. They can also be used in marinades and dressings.

Lychees These fruits have gleaming white, occasionally pink, juicy flesh covering a shiny, coffee-coloured seed. Sweet and fragrant, they make a refreshing snack.

Longans This fruit comes in several varieties. The Chinese set much store by dried longan as a sweet ingredient in herbal drinks.

Mandarin oranges These symbolize the gift of prosperity during the Lunar New Year. They are eaten fresh, or dried to add a citrus flavour to many savoury stews and sweet dishes.

Mangoes The sweet, juicy, yellow or orange flesh is thirst-quenching, with a delightful aroma of pine.

Papayas The ripe, yellow-skinned, gourd-like papaya with its flame-coloured flesh is sweet and full of vitamins.

Persimmons Also known as sharon fruit, these are grown widely in south China. Dried persimmon has been an integral ingredient in Chinese cooking for centuries, especially in herbal drinks.

Below, left to right **Mangetouts, tofu skins, spring onions, dried tofu.**

Pineapples These sweet, juicy fruits are mainly eaten fresh as a dessert, and are also used in sweet and sour dishes.

Plums Chinese plums are eaten fresh or pickled, dried, salted or puréed into plum sauce. Salted or candied plums are a favourite snack throughout China.

Star fruits (carambolas) This pretty fruit has a mildly floral flavour, similar to an Asian pear, but juicier. In south China it is often dried and salted to be enjoyed as a snack. The green immature fruit is often sliced and served as part of a salad or added to stir-fries.

Above, left to right Mango, bananas, *Mui Kwai Lo*, green tea.

Beverages

Tea is the main non-alcoholic beverage of south China, although Chinese wine made from grains is also a popular drink, especially when served warm.

Alcoholic drinks Archaeological digs in China can date the existence of alcohol as far back as 4,000 years; certainly by the 11th century wine-making from fruits and grains was a countrywide industry.

Broadly, Chinese wines come under two headings – yellow and white grain liquor. The two main varieties are made from glutinous rice and are fermented (*huang jiu* – yellow liquor) and distilled (*mi jiu* – white liquor). White liquor is commonly called *shaojiu* or 'burned liquor', either because of the sensation it produces in the mouth or the fact that it is usually served warm.

There are many types of flavoured wines used in the cooking of southern China. *Wu Liang Ye* (five-grain liquor) is a heady spirit; the five grains are sorghum, rice, glutinous rice, sweet corn and unhusked wheat. *To Mei Jau* is a Cantonese liquor produced from rice wine, with added *to mei*, a flower found locally, and crystal sugar syrup. *Mui Kwai Lo* is rose-flavoured and aromatic. Sweet sherry makes a good substitute.

Tea

Although there are hundreds of varieties of tea, they all fall into two basic categories, black (sometimes called red) and green. Both types come from the same plant and the chief differences lie in processing. Black tea is first fermented, or oxidized, which is the technical term for this process. When it is only semi-fermented, or semi-oxidized, it is called *Oolong* tea. The name is derived from *Wu Long*, meaning 'black dragon', and the strongest of these is *Tie Guan Yin*, meaning 'iron goddess of mercy'. Green tea is unfermented and is dried in the sun or in special drying kilns, where the leaves may also be steamed to make them soft. They are then rolled and fired in the kilns until they turn a yellowish-green and take on their unique curled shape. The finest teas are still hand-processed, especially the rare teas such as Gunpowder and Dragon Well.

Soups

Incredibly versatile, Chinese soups can be dressed up or down, served as an individual portion or on the side, or take centre stage as a communal offering. However they are presented, they are always prepared with a firm eye on how complementary they are to other dishes served at the same time. If the meal features meat or poultry dishes and stir-fried vegetables, then the soup will counterbalance these elements. This adheres to the ancient yin-yang tenet of perfect harmony.

Rib-stickers and palate cleansers

There is one fundamental difference between the Chinese meal structure and that of other cuisines: soups are rarely, if ever, served as stand-alone appetizers at the start of a meal. Soups are nonetheless very important in Cantonese food philosophy and according to a traditional saying they are thought to 'smoothen the soul'.

There are various types of soup on offer in the region. Light ones, such as clear Egg Drop and Ginger Soup, with a hint of Chinese wine, are often served as an accompaniment and designed to refresh the palate between helpings of other dishes. Other, more robust brews, such as Beef Ball Soup and Liver and Matrimony Vine Soup, contain substantial ingredients like fish and meat. These make good meal-in-one options when circumstances or lack of time demand less kitchen work and, therefore, uncomplicated, quick meals.

Seafood and meat dumplings often feature in soups that are served specifically to complement rice or noodle dishes. Prawn Wonton Soup is a case in point, and is served whenever Chilli Noodles are on the menu, making for a well-balanced meal.

Serves 4

750ml/1¼ pints/3 cups fresh
  vegetable stock
30ml/2 tbsp fresh root ginger,
  finely shredded
2 eggs
30ml/2 tbsp Chinese wine
chopped spring onions (scallions)
  or fresh coriander (cilantro),
  to garnish

Egg drop and ginger soup

The name of this dish is a literal one, as you physically drop the egg into the boiling stock where it forms long strands. The soup is very easy to make, nutritious and beautifully light; the sort of thing that would be served at home to refresh the palate between more elaborate dishes.

1 Bring the stock to the boil in a medium pan. Add the finely shredded ginger and cook for 3 minutes.

2 Meanwhile, beat the eggs in a bowl or jug (pitcher). Pour them into the boiling soup in a steady stream, using a fork or chopsticks to stir the surface at the same time. As it cooks, the egg will set, forming long shreds or strands.

3 Stir in the rice wine. Ladle into bowls, garnish with the spring onions or coriander, and serve hot.

Variation For more substance, soak a handful of cellophane noodles in boiling water for 5 minutes. Drain and add to the soup just before dropping in the egg. This version is filling enough to serve as a complete light meal.

Per portion Energy 44kcal/184kJ; Protein 3.3g; Carbohydrate 0.2g, of which sugars 0.1g; Fat 2.9g, of which saturates 0.8g; Cholesterol 95mg; Calcium 18mg; Fibre 0.1g; Sodium 166mg.

Liver and matrimony vine soup

Matrimony vine also goes by the name of boxthorn on account of the sharp thorns at the base of each leaf stalk. Only the spinach-like leaves are eaten; the stems are discarded. Legend has it that if boxthorn is planted close to a house, marital discord will follow – hence the name 'matrimony vine'.

1 Put the liver in the freezer for about 10 minutes, until it is firm enough to slice very finely with a sharp knife.

2 Meanwhile, prepare the matrimony vine. Pull the leaves away from the stems, taking care to avoid the thorns. Wash the leaves thoroughly under plenty of cold running water and drain them in a colander.

3 Pour the stock into a large pan and bring to the boil. Add the ginger, soy sauce, pepper and sesame oil.

4 Add the matrimony vine leaves to the pan, simmer for 2 minutes, then add the sliced liver. Cook for 2 minutes more, until the liver is just cooked. Ladle the soup into warm bowls and serve immediately.

Serves 4

200g/7oz pig's liver
4–6 stalks of matrimony vine
750ml/1¼ pints/3 cups fresh
  vegetable stock
30ml/2 tbsp fresh root ginger,
  finely shredded
30ml/2 tbsp light soy sauce
2.5ml/½ tsp ground black pepper
30ml/2 tbsp sesame oil

Cook's tip Matrimony vine is called gow gei in Cantonese and is sold in most Chinese stores. The plant also yields wolf or goji berries, which are claimed to have rejuvenating powers. Handle it with care, as the thorns at the base of the leaves are very sharp.

Variation If you cannot locate matrimony vine, use young spinach leaves instead.

Per portion Energy 113kcal/472kJ; Protein 11.3g; Carbohydrate 0.9g, of which sugars 0.9g; Fat 7.2g, of which saturates 1.3g; Cholesterol 130mg; Calcium 31mg; Fibre 0.4g; Sodium 600mg.

Prawn wonton soup

The light stock for this wonton soup derives its richness from dried fish like sprats or anchovies. While Chinese stores sell instant wonton soup stock, it is easier – and more satisfying – to make your own. Extra flavour comes from the wontons, which are filled with a delicious seafood mixture.

1 Start by preparing the wonton filling. Chop the prawns finely to make a coarse paste. This can be done in a food processor, but make sure you use the pulse button, or the prawns will become rubbery.

2 Scrape the chopped prawns into a bowl and add the soy sauce, sesame oil, pepper and cornflour. Mix well. Place about 5ml/1 tsp of the mixture in the centre of a wonton wrapper, bring the edges together so that they meet at the top, and pinch the neck to seal. Fill the remaining wontons in the same way.

3 Bring a small pan of water to the boil. Add the wontons and cook them for 5 minutes. Drain in a colander, transfer to a bowl and toss with a light dribble of oil to prevent them from sticking together.

4 Put the dried sprats or anchovies in a large pan. Pour in the water, add the soy sauce and bring to the boil. Cook for 5 minutes. Taste and add more soy sauce if needed. Strain the soup, return it to the pan and heat through.

5 Place four wontons in each warmed soup bowl. Ladle the soup over, garnish with the spring onions and serve.

Variation For a vegetarian version, use chopped mushrooms instead of prawns (shrimp) in the filling, and make the stock using dried mushrooms instead of the dried fish.

Serves 4

60g/2oz dried sprats or anchovies
750ml/1¼ pints/3 cups water
15ml/1 tbsp light soy sauce
chopped spring onions (scallions),
  to garnish

For the wontons
300g/11oz raw prawns (shrimp),
  peeled and deveined
15ml/1 tbsp light soy sauce
15ml/1 tbsp sesame oil
2.5ml/½ tsp ground black pepper
15ml/1 tbsp cornflour (cornstarch)
16 wonton wrappers

Per portion Energy 178kcal/748kJ; Protein 19g; Carbohydrate 15.2g, of which sugars 0.8g; Fat 4.9g, of which saturates 0.8g; Cholesterol 156mg; Calcium 132mg; Fibre 0.6g; Sodium 1267mg.

Stuffed squid soup

Squid enjoys an honourable position in the Cantonese kitchen. Chefs have innumerable ways of preparing it: in stir-fried and deep-fried dishes, as a major ingredient in noodle dishes and in a range of soups. This dish typifies the Cantonese genius for combining seafood and meat.

1 Put the noodles in a bowl and pour over just-boiled water to cover. Soak for 20 minutes, or until the noodles have softened.

2 Prepare each squid by cutting off the tentacles just below the eye. Remove the transparent 'quill' from inside the body and rub off the skin on the outside. Wash the squid thoroughly in cold water, drain and set aside on a plate.

3 Put the pork in a bowl. Add the cornflour, sesame oil, spring onions, pepper and fish sauce. Mix well.

4 Stuff each squid three quarters full with the pork mixture. Do not use more, as the squid will shrink when cooked, and the filling may pop out.

5 Pour the stock into a pan that will hold the squid comfortably and bring to the boil. Add the squid and cook for 5 minutes.

6 Drain the noodles and add them to the pan. Cook for 2 minutes more. Serve in warmed bowls, garnished with the preserved turnip and a grinding of black pepper.

Cook's tips
• Cellophane noodles go by various names, including mung bean noodles, transparent noodles, bean thread noodles and glass noodles.
• Preserved turnip (tung chye) is sold in Chinese food stores. It is crunchy and slightly sweet, and goes very well with fish.

Serves 4

50g/2oz cellophane noodles
8 medium squid
150g/5oz/⅔ cup minced
  (ground) pork
5ml/1 tsp cornflour (cornstarch)
15ml/1 tbsp sesame oil
15ml/1 tbsp finely chopped spring
  onions (scallions)
5ml/1 tsp ground black pepper
15ml/1 tbsp fish sauce
750ml/1¼ pints/3 cups fresh
  fish stock
15ml/1 tbsp preserved turnip
  (*see* Cook's tip)

Per portion Energy 279kcal/1175kJ; Protein 34.9g; Carbohydrate 13.7g, of which sugars 0.3g; Fat 9.4g, of which saturates 2.5g; Cholesterol 419mg; Calcium 31mg; Fibre 0.2g; Sodium 220mg.

Chicken broth of prosperity

The origin of this popular dish is rather obscure. Like many dishes that grace the family table in China, especially during celebrations such as Chinese New Year, the ingredients are imbued with symbolic meaning. Ham and quail's eggs suggest the wealth and prosperity alluded to in the title, while the chicken represents the legendary phoenix, a symbol of rebirth that is particularly appropriate at the start of a new year. This flavoursome soup is very substantial and nutritious, and is sometimes so thick that it can be served on plates rather than in bowls.

1 Cook the quail's eggs in a pan of boiling water for 8 minutes. Drain, refresh under cold water and remove the shells. Set the eggs aside.

2 Pour the chicken stock into a large pan and bring to the boil. Add the chicken breast fillets, lower the heat slightly and simmer for 10 minutes or until cooked through. Using tongs, lift them out of the pan and leave to cool.

3 Add the ham to the pan of stock and simmer for 15 minutes. Meanwhile, cut the chicken into shreds.

4 Add the sesame oil, soy sauce and pepper to the ham and stock mixture. Simmer gently for 2 minutes, then add the shredded chicken and beaten eggs, stirring all the time so that the eggs form strands. Simmer for 2 minutes.

5 Stir in the cornflour paste. Continue to stir until the soup thickens, then add the shelled quail's eggs and heat through for 1–2 minutes. Ladle into warm bowls and serve.

Serves 4

4 quail's eggs
750ml/1¼ pints/3 cups fresh
  chicken stock
2 chicken breast fillets
150g/5oz Chinese or Serrano ham,
  finely diced
30ml/2 tbsp sesame oil
30ml/2 tbsp light soy sauce
2.5ml/½ tsp ground black pepper
2 eggs, lightly beaten
30ml/2 tbsp cornflour (cornstarch)
  mixed to a paste with 60ml/4 tbsp
  cold water

Per portion Energy 254kcal/1065kJ; Protein 29.9g; Carbohydrate 7.9g, of which sugars 0.9g; Fat 11.8g, of which saturates 2.6g; Cholesterol 217mg; Calcium 31mg; Fibre 0g; Sodium 1086mg.

Beef ball soup

Many southern Chinese do not eat beef as they regard the cow as a sacred animal, without which they would not be able to till the soil on their farms. The Hakka people, being seafarers by tradition, do not subscribe to this bovine reverence and happily cook this sustaining beef soup, with its richly perfumed and flavoursome stock.

1 Chop the beef into small cubes and process in a blender or food processor until smooth. Add the cornflour, 5ml/1 tsp salt and ground black pepper and continue to blend the mixture until it has the consistency of smooth pâté.

2 Scrape the meat mixture into a bowl and shape it into small balls, each the size of a large cherry tomato. When you process meat for a long time, it takes on a springy texture that is a little chewy when cooked.

3 Pour the beef stock into a large pan. Bring to the boil and add the onion, star anise, cloves, cinnamon stick, peppercorns and remaining salt. Lower the heat and simmer for 20 minutes. Using a slotted spoon, remove the onion and whole spices.

4 Bring the stock to the boil again. Add the beef balls and cook them for 5 minutes. Ladle the soup into warm bowls and give each portion an equal number of beef balls. Garnish with coriander and serve immediately.

Cook's tip The meat needs to be very finely processed so this would be difficult to make without a food processor. Many Chinese stores sell the beef balls ready made, which is a great time-saver. Simply make the stock, drop in the meatballs and cook for a few minutes.

Serves 4

400g/14oz beef sirloin
15ml/1 tbsp cornflour (cornstarch)
15ml/3 tsp salt
5ml/1 tsp ground black pepper
1 litre/1¾ pints/4 cups fresh
  beef stock
1 large onion, sliced
2 star anise
6 cloves
1 x 10cm/4in cinnamon stick
5ml/1 tsp black peppercorns
chopped coriander (cilantro),
  to serve

Per portion Energy 247kcal/1031kJ; Protein 24.3g; Carbohydrate 16.8g, of which sugars 7g; Fat 9.6g, of which saturates 3.8g; Cholesterol 58mg; Calcium 38mg; Fibre 1.8g; Sodium 1546mg.

Dim sum

Literally meaning 'food to touch the heart', dim sum are immensely popular throughout China and the rest of the world. The evolution of this Cantonese way of eating since its ancient beginnings in Guangdong is closely connected with the Chinese penchant for consuming light snacks with tea. This led to a huge increase in demand and, over the centuries since 200BC, chefs from all over China have been challenged to be ever more inventive in preparing bitesize morsels, dumplings, snacks and assorted finger food.

Moist morsels and crunchy bites

Dim sum were never meant to provide a full meal, and favourites such as *cha siew bau* (Roast Pork Dumplings), *shao mai* (Minced Pork Dumplings) and savoury cakes made from root vegetables were originally served much like Spanish tapas – as a light snack.

Over time, however, the range has grown and today eating dim sum invariably mean consuming an eclectic variety of small dishes that can comprise a full meal. Dim sum restaurants sprang up to meet the growing demand for this type of dining and are now the venue of choice for people all over the world.

Each region of China makes use of indigenous ingredients, resulting in dishes like Crystal Dumplings, made with special translucent skins. Seasonings, on the other hand, remain within the classic Cantonese canon of black bean sauce, hoisin sauce, sesame oil, garlic and spring onions (scallions).

Fried or steamed, wrapped with rice or wheat flour batters, there is a growing cornucopia of new types of dim sum joining the tried-and-tested repertoire. As a meal for one or ten, the most appealing element is that you eat what you like from the dim sum trolley and are not dictated to by a rigid menu.

Yam cake

The vegetable on which this Cantonese classic is based inevitably causes confusion. In America it is called taro, where yam can refer to an orange-fleshed sweet potato. To muddy the waters still further, there is a Chinese vegetable called yam bean, but that is different again. What you want for this classic recipe is the large barrel-shaped vegetable with a hairy brown skin and purple-flecked flesh. Alternatively, you could use pumpkin.

1 Put the dried shrimp in a bowl and pour over water to cover. Soak for 1 hour, until soft. Heat the oil in a frying pan and fry the shallots for 4–5 minutes, until brown and crisp. Lift out with a slotted spoon and set aside.

2 Drain the soaked shrimp and chop them roughly. Reheat the oil remaining in the pan and fry the shrimp with the diced sausage for 3 minutes. Transfer the shrimp and sausage to a bowl and set aside.

3 Peel the yam and remove the fibrous stalk. Cut the flesh into large chunks and place in a steamer placed over simmering water. Steam for 20 minutes until the flesh is soft.

4 Put the yam into a large bowl and mash with a potato masher. Stir in the rice flour and the tapioca or cornflour, then add the water and salt. Mix well.

5 Set aside 30ml/2 tbsp of the fried shallots. Add the remainder to the shrimp mixture. Stir in the spring onions, soy sauce, sesame oil and pepper. Fry gently in a hot wok for 2 minutes so that the flavours combine.

6 Add the mixture to the mashed yams. Mix well, then press into a lightly oiled steaming tray. Sprinkle the reserved fried shallots over the surface. Steam over rapidly boiling water for 15 minutes. Cool, then cut into wedges, garnish with the reserved fried shallots and spring onions, and serve with the chilli dipping sauce.

Serves 6–8

50g/2oz dried shrimp
75ml/5 tbsp vegetable oil
15 shallots, thinly sliced
2 Chinese sausages, diced finely
1 kg/2¼lb yam (taro)
300g/11oz/2 cups rice flour
115g/4oz/1 cup tapioca flour
  or 115g/4oz/1 cup cornflour
  (cornstarch)
750ml/1¼ pints/2 cups water
5ml/1 tsp salt
2 spring onions (scallions), plus
  extra, chopped, to garnish
30ml/2 tbsp light soy sauce
30ml/2 tbsp sesame oil
2.5ml/½ tsp ground black pepper
chilli dipping sauce, for serving

Cook's tip Dried shrimp are sold in most Chinese food stores. They have a very strong smell, but this dissipates when they are cooked.

Per portion Energy 481kcal/2025kJ; Protein 9.9g; Carbohydrate 79.6g, of which sugars 2.6g; Fat 14.6g, of which saturates 2.9g; Cholesterol 37mg; Calcium 121mg; Fibre 3g; Sodium 648mg.

Radish cake

Closely related to yam cake, this recipe makes innovative use of the large white radish that is also known as mooli or daikon. As a vegetable, white radish is fairly bland, although it is useful for making soup stock. Process it to a paste and mix it with rice flour, however, and it is magically transformed.

1 Put the dried shrimp in a bowl and pour over water to cover. Soak for 1 hour, until soft.

2 Meanwhile, peel the radish and chop it roughly. Process it in batches in a blender or food processor to a soft white purée. Scrape into a strainer and press down with a spoon to extract as much liquid as possible. Tip the radish purée into a bowl and stir in the rice flour and the tapioca or cornflour. Add the water and salt. Mix well.

3 Drain the soaked shrimp and chop them roughly. Spoon the radish purée into a non-stick pan and cook over low heat, stirring frequently, for 5 minutes.

4 Heat the vegetable oil in a frying pan or wok. Add the chopped shrimp and fry for 2 minutes, then add the radish purée. Stir well, then add the soy sauce, sesame oil and black pepper. Mix thoroughly to combine.

5 Press the mixture into a lightly oiled steaming tray. Steam over a pan of rapidly boiling water for 20 minutes. Set aside. When cold, slice into bite-size pieces and serve plain or with a dipping sauce of your choice.

Cook's tips
• White radishes are much larger than the more common red variety and can weigh up to 1kg/2¼lb. Choose ones that are pearly white and firm, as old radishes become fibrous.
• Radish cake can be frozen and thawed without losing any of its flavour.

Serves 6–8

50g/2oz dried shrimp
1kg/2¼lb white radish,
   (also called mooli or daikon)
300g/11oz/2 cups rice flour
115g/4oz/1 cup tapioca flour
   or 115g/4oz/1 cup cornflour
   (cornstarch)
750ml/1¼ pints/3 cups water
5ml/1 tsp salt
30ml/2 tbsp vegetable oil
30ml/2 tbsp light soy sauce
30ml/2 tbsp sesame oil
2.5ml/½ tsp ground black pepper
dipping sauce, optional,
   to serve

Variation The pieces of cold radish cake can be fried lightly in oil before being served.

Per portion Energy 263kcal/1099kJ; Protein 7g; Carbohydrate 44.2g, of which sugars 2.7g; Fat 6.3g, of which saturates 0.9g; Cholesterol 32mg; Calcium 111mg; Fibre 1.9g; Sodium 560mg.

Braised beancurd skin parcels

Beancurd skins are a healthier option than wheat-flour-based spring roll wrappers and taste much better, especially when they have a delicious chicken, mushroom and bean sauce filling. These little parcels do not take long to steam, and make an excellent addition to a selection of dim sum.

1 Soak the mushrooms in a bowl of boiling water for 20–30 minutes, until soft. Drain and slice into thin strips, discarding the stems. Slice the chicken into 1cm/½in thick strips.

2 Heat the vegetable oil in a wok or frying pan. Add the chicken and mushroom strips and stir-fry for 3 minutes. Add the black bean sauce, pepper, sugar and sesame oil and stir-fry for 2 minutes more.

3 Pour in the water. Cook over high heat until most of it has been driven off and the mixture is thick and almost dry. Transfer to a bowl and leave to cool.

4 Place a beancurd skin on a clean, flat surface or chopping board and cut into pieces about 10cm/4in wide. Top with two or three pieces each of chicken and mushroom, tuck in the edges and roll up to make a parcel about 6cm/2½in long. Fill the other skins in the same way.

5 Place the beancurd skin parcels on a large plate and steam over a wok of rapidly boiling water for 10 minutes. Serve hot.

Cook's tips

• Dried beancurd skins are usually sold in large sheets. Check that they are not brittle or cracked, which would suggest they had been sitting too long on the grocer's shelf. Good beancurd skins should be soft and pliable. If the beancurd skins are a little brittle, dampen a clean dish towel and place it over them for 5 minutes.

• Any unused skins should be packed flat in plastic bags, and sealed tightly. Keep in a dry larder but do not put in the refrigerator as dry cold air makes them brittle.

Serves 4

4 dried Chinese black mushrooms
300g/11oz chicken breast fillet
30ml/2 tbsp vegetable oil
30ml/2 tbsp black bean sauce
2.5ml/½ tsp ground black pepper
2.5ml/½ tsp sugar
30ml/2 tbsp sesame oil
100ml/3½fl oz/scant ½ cup water
1–2 sheets of beancurd skins

Variations Add a few pieces of finely shredded ginger to the filling for a spicy touch. The mushroom soaking liquid can be strained and used in place of some or all of the water in the filling.

Per portion Energy 188kcal/785kJ; Protein 18.6g; Carbohydrate 1.9g, of which sugars 0.6g; Fat 11.9g, of which saturates 1.7g; Cholesterol 53mg; Calcium 7mg; Fibre 0.2g; Sodium 46mg.

Crystal dumplings

A much-loved street food, these dumplings are often sold by vendors carrying their wares in two baskets slung either side of a long bamboo pole. Called chui kuay *(water dumplings) by the Swatow-speaking Shantou people on account of their translucent skins, they are especially delicious with a sweet soy sauce and chilli dip.*

1 Put the sweet potato flour in a non-stick pan. Add the water and oil and cook over low heat, stirring occasionally, until thick. Remove from the heat and leave to cool for 15 minutes.

2 Meanwhile, shred the bamboo shoots for the filling until they are more or less the shape and size of beansprouts. Put them in a colander, rinse thoroughly and drain.

3 Heat the oil in a wok and fry the garlic over low heat for 40 seconds. Do not let it burn. Add the bamboo shoots, soy sauce, oyster sauce, pepper and water. Cook over medium heat for 10 minutes, until the mixture is almost dry. Remove from the heat and leave to cool.

4 Stir the tapioca flour into the cool sweet potato flour mixture. Mix well, then transfer to a floured board. Knead for at least 5 minutes, punching the dough as you roll and fold. This makes it very light. Shape the dough into a long roll, about 5cm/2in in diameter. Slice off pieces 9mm/⅜in thick and flatten each with a rolling pin to form very thin, unbroken circles.

5 Place about 30ml/2 tbsp bamboo shoots on each dough circle, fold over into a half-moon shape and seal the edges. Trim off any excess dough and fold and pinch until you get a serrated edge on each dumpling.

6 Place the dumplings on a lightly oiled plate and steam over a wok of rapidly boiling water for 30 minutes, topping up the water as necessary.

7 Meanwhile, mix together all the ingredients for the sweet soy sauce and chilli dip in a small bowl. Transfer to a serving bowl. Serve the dumplings warm with the dip.

Serves 6–8

200g/7oz/1¾ cups sweet
  potato flour
400ml/14fl oz/1⅔ cups water
30ml/2 tbsp vegetable oil
115g/4oz/1 cup tapioca flour

For the filling
400g/14oz can bamboo
  shoots, drained
45ml/3 tbsp vegetable oil
3 garlic cloves, crushed
30ml/2 tbsp dark soy sauce
30ml/2 tbsp oyster sauce
5ml/1 tsp ground black pepper
200ml/7fl oz/scant 1 cup water

Sweet Soy Sauce and Chilli Dip
45ml/3 tbsp dark soy sauce
15ml/1 tbsp ginger purée
15ml/1 tbsp rice vinegar
15ml/1 tbsp sesame oil
5ml/1 tsp sugar
5ml/1 tsp chilli bean paste

Per portion Energy 244kcal/1022kJ; Protein 3.6g;
Carbohydrate 38.2g, of which sugars 5.2g; Fat 8.7g,
of which saturates 1.1g; Cholesterol 0mg; Calcium
21mg; Fibre 1.3g; Sodium 1134mg.

Chive dumplings

These dumplings are lovely and light, thanks to the wheat starch flour used for the wrappers. Although there is an art to making them, the end result is well worth the effort. Some versions feature a filling of bamboo shoots or sweet Chinese turnips, but the Chinese chives used in this recipe add crunch and flavour. These are different from regular chives, being flatter and broader and with a distinctive, fresh aroma.

1 Put the wheat starch in a non-stick pan. Add the water and oil and cook over low heat, stirring occasionally, until very thick. Remove from the heat and leave to cool for 15 minutes.

2 Meanwhile, prepare the filling. Chop the chives finely. Put them in a bowl and stir in the soy sauce, sesame oil, pepper and cornflour. Heat a wok, add the mixture and toss over low heat for 5 minutes. Stir in the lightly beaten egg to bind the mixture, then set it aside.

3 Stir the tapioca flour and salt into the cool wheat starch mixture. Mix well, then transfer to a floured board. Knead for at least 5 minutes. Roll out the dough and stamp out into 12 circles, 7.5cm/3in in diameter.

4 Place 1 heaped tablespoon of the filling on each dough circle and fold to make half-moon shapes. Seal the edges with a little water. Brush each dumpling with a little sesame oil to prevent them from sticking together when being steamed.

5 Place the dumplings on a plate and steam over rapidly boiling water for 10 minutes. Serve immediately, with a chilli sauce dip.

Cook's tip Wheat starch has a very fine consistency, similar to that of cornflour (cornstarch), which you can use if you can't find wheat starch, but it is especially good for making dim sum dough. It is widely available in Chinese stores.

Serves 6–8

150g/5oz/1¼ cups wheat starch
200ml/7fl oz/scant 1 cup water
15ml/1 tbsp vegetable oil
50g/2oz/½ cup tapioca flour
pinch of salt
sesame oil, for brushing
  the dumplings
chilli sauce, for dipping

For the filling
200g/7oz Chinese chives
30ml/2 tbsp light soy sauce
15ml/1 tbsp sesame oil
2.5ml/½ tsp ground black pepper
15ml/1 tbsp cornflour (cornstarch)
1 egg, lightly beaten

Per portion Energy 140kcal/589kJ; Protein 1.8g; Carbohydrate 25.9g, of which sugars 0.9g; Fat 3.9g, of which saturates 0.6g; Cholesterol 24mg; Calcium 58mg; Fibre 1.3g; Sodium 295mg.

Pork and nut dumplings

These dainty little bites use basically the same dough as for chive dumplings, but their taste and texture is totally different. This is thanks to the unusual filling, with its interplay of succulent pork, crunchy nuts and aromatics. These are a typical Shantou dim sum.

1 Put the wheat starch in a non-stick pan. Add the water and oil and cook over low heat, stirring occasionally, until very thick. Remove from the heat and leave to cool for 15 minutes.

2 Meanwhile, make the filling. Heat the oil in a small pan and fry the pork for 2 minutes. Add the water, chopped peanuts, soy sauce, sesame oil and ground black pepper. Stir for 3 minutes until the pork is cooked through and there is the barest hint of sauce. Set aside to cool.

3 Stir the tapioca flour and salt into the cool wheat starch mixture. Mix well, then transfer to a floured board. Knead for at least 5 minutes. Divide into 12 portions. Flatten each piece of dough and roll them into 7.5cm/3in circles.

4 Place 1 heaped tablespoon of the filling on each dough circle and fold to make half-moon shapes. Seal the edges with a little water. Brush each dumpling with a little sesame oil to prevent them from sticking together when being steamed.

5 Place the dumplings on a large plate and steam over a wok of rapidly boiling water for 10 minutes.

6 Meanwhile, mix together all the ingredients for the Black Vinegar and Ginger Dip in a small bowl. Transfer to a serving bowl. Serve the dumplings hot, with the dipping sauce.

Cook's tip Small versions of these dumplings make excellent appetizers, especially when served with the Black Vinegar and Ginger Dip.

Serves 6–8

150g/5oz/1¼ cups wheat starch
200ml/7fl oz/scant 1 cup water
15ml/1 tbsp vegetable oil
50g/2oz/½ cup tapioca flour or
  cornflour (cornstarch)
pinch of salt

For the filling
30ml/2 tbsp vegetable oil
200g/7oz/scant 1 cup minced
  (ground) pork
90ml/6 tbsp water
50g/2oz/½ cup peanuts, chopped
30ml/2 tbsp light soy sauce
15ml/1 tbsp sesame oil
2.5ml/½ tsp black pepper

Black Vinegar and Ginger Dip
45ml/3 tbsp black vinegar
5ml/1 tbsp finely shredded
  fresh root ginger
small pinch of salt

Per portion Energy 216kcal/906kJ; Protein 6.7g;
Carbohydrate 24.3g, of which sugars 0.7g; Fat 10.9g,
of which saturates 2.1g; Cholesterol 17mg; Calcium
10mg; Fibre 0.4g; Sodium 294mg.

Roast pork dumplings

Known as char siew bau *in Cantonese, these quintessential dim sum delicacies owe their excellence to a trade secret that has long eluded the common cook. The secret lies in the special low gluten flour that makes these dumplings light, white and fluffy, which is called* dai garn fun *in Cantonese and is available in Chinese food stores.*

1 Put the flour and salt in a large mixing bowl and sprinkle in the yeast. Make a well in the centre and pour in the warm water and vinegar. Mix to a dough.

2 Place the dough on a floured board and knead for 10 minutes. Return it to the bowl, cover and set aside in a warm place to rise for 20 minutes or until it has doubled in bulk.

3 Knock back (punch down) the dough, knead it again, return it to the bowl and set aside in a warm place for 15 minutes.

4 Meanwhile, make the filling. Put the diced pork in a bowl. Stir in the hoisin sauce to moisten it, then add the spring onion.

5 Roll out the dough on a floured board and shape it into a 30cm/12in long roll, about 5cm/2in in diameter. Cut the roll into 2.5 cm/1in slices and flatten each of these with a rolling pin to a thin round, about 9cm/3½in across.

6 Holding a pastry round on the palm of one hand, spoon a heaped teaspoon of the filling into the centre. Cup your hand so that the dough enfolds the filling, pleating and pinching it where necessary. Pinch off the excess dough at the top and seal with a twisting action. Fill the remaining dumplings in the same way.

7 Cut 5cm/2in squares of baking parchment. Stand a dumpling on each piece of paper in a steamer. Steam for 15 minutes. Serve immediately.

Makes 12

200g/7oz/1¾ cups low gluten flour
 (*dai garn fun*)
pinch of salt
5ml/1 tsp easy-blend (rapid-rise)
 dried yeast
120ml/4fl oz/½ cup warm water
5ml/1 tsp vinegar

For the filling
115g/4oz cold roast pork,
 finely diced
30ml/2 tbsp hoisin sauce
1 spring onion (scallion),
 finely chopped

Cook's tip Don't throw away the bits of pastry you pinch off the top of the dumplings. Rolled together, they will yield enough dough for two more dumplings.

Per portion Energy 73kcal/309kJ; Protein 2.4g; Carbohydrate 15.6g, of which sugars 0.2g; Fat 0.5g, of which saturates 0.2g; Cholesterol 6mg; Calcium 4mg; Fibre 0g; Sodium 194mg.

Pork and prawn dumplings

While dim sum are generally attributed to southern China, these bitesize morsels, called shao mai, *are enjoyed throughout the entire country. Pork is the main ingredient in the filling used here, but there are also seafood versions.*

1 Chop the prawns finely to make a coarse paste. This can be done using a sharp knife or in a food processor, but if you use a food processor use the pulse button, or the prawns will become rubbery. Scrape into a bowl.

2 Chop the spring onions very finely. Add them to the puréed prawns, with the pork, soy sauce, sesame oil, pepper and cornflour. Mix well.

3 Holding a wonton wrapper on the palm of one hand, spoon a heaped teaspoon of the filling into the centre. Cup your hand so that the wrapper enfolds the filling to make the classic dumpling shape. Leave the top slightly open. Top each gap with a pea. Fill the remaining wonton wrappers in the same way.

4 Place the dumplings on a lightly oiled plate and steam over a wok of rapidly boiling water for 10 minutes. Serve with a chilli sauce dip.

Serves 4

100g/3¾oz raw prawns (shrimp), peeled and deveined
2 spring onions (scallions)
225g/8oz/1 cup minced (ground) pork
30ml/2 tbsp light soy sauce
15ml/1 tbsp sesame oil
2.5ml/½ tsp ground black pepper
15ml/1 tbsp cornflour (cornstarch)
16 round wonton wrappers
16 large garden peas, thawed if frozen
chilli sauce, for dipping

Cook's tip If you can only find square wonton wrappers, trim off the corners to make a rough circle before filling them.

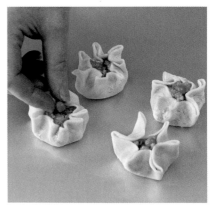

Per portion Energy 228kcal/957kJ; Protein 18.2g; Carbohydrate 20.2g, of which sugars 1.3g; Fat 8.8g, of which saturates 2.5g; Cholesterol 86mg; Calcium 57mg; Fibre 1.3g; Sodium 622mg.

Deep-fried wontons

These are a close cousin of shao mai *(pork dumplings). They have much the same ingredients but are fried rather than steamed. Crisp on the outside, with a tender filling, it may be an idea to make double the quantity.*

1 Put the minced pork in a bowl. Add the light soy sauce, sesame oil, ground black pepper and cornflour. Mix well.

2 Place about 5ml/1 tsp of the mixture in the centre of a wonton wrapper, bring the corners together so that they meet at the top, and pinch the neck to seal. Fill the remaining wontons in the same way.

3 Heat the oil in a wok or deep-fryer. Carefully add the filled wontons, about four or five at a time, and deep-fry until golden brown.

4 Carefully lift out the cooked wontons with a slotted spoon, drain on kitchen paper and keep hot while frying successive batches. Serve the wontons hot with chilli dipping sauce or plum sauce.

Variations For seafood wontons, use finely chopped crab, scallops or prawns (shrimp) in place of the pork. These can be served hot or cold.

Serves 4

300g/11oz/1½ cups minced
  (ground) pork
15ml/1 tbsp light soy sauce
15ml/1 tbsp sesame oil
2.5ml/½ tsp ground black pepper
15ml/1 tbsp cornflour (cornstarch)
16 wonton wrappers
vegetable oil for deep-frying
chilli dipping sauce or plum sauce,
  to serve

Cook's tips

• If the wonton skins are brittle, wipe them with a damp towel or they will be difficult to shape without cracking.
• Filled wontons take very little time to cook. Make sure your oil is not too hot as they scorch very quickly.

Per portion Energy 326kcal/1357kJ; Protein 16.3g; Carbohydrate 18.3g, of which sugars 0.6g; Fat 21.3g, of which saturates 4.4g; Cholesterol 50mg; Calcium 33mg; Fibre 0.6g; Sodium 319mg.

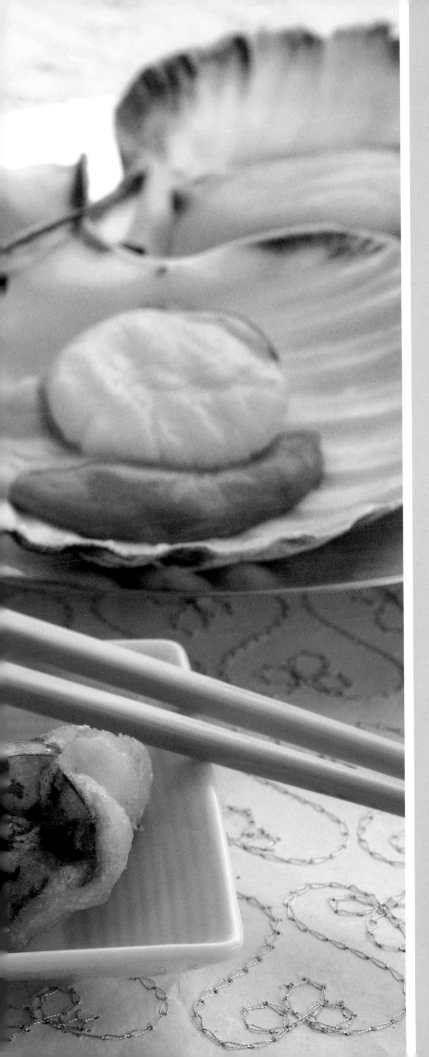

Fish and shellfish

As much of south China's inland rivers, coastal regions and islands abound with good things to eat, the availability of top-quality fresh seafood has never been a problem in the region. Perhaps because of its ready availability, fish has always been accorded a prized place within every meal in the region, its intrinsic flavour and texture cleverly brought out by skilful cooking. In accordance with the Taoist belief that no living creature should go to the next world with missing parts, most fish are cooked and served whole, with a range of other ingredients.

Simple flavours and tender flesh

The preparation of fish and shellfish in southern Chinese cooking is governed by what the resultant taste will be when it has been cooked. Sweet and Sour Snapper and Braised Carp are perfect examples of this, as great care is taken both to cook the fish and create the aromatic sauces that accompany them. Delicate freshwater fish is steamed in Shantou or Fujian style, with just a hint of ginger and sour plums. More robust seafood, such as prawns (shrimp), are often served with rich tomato or oyster sauces, resulting in dishes like Red Cooked Prawns on the Shell.

Shellfish are plentiful on the shores off Hainan Island and the signature dish here is called Wenchang Steamed Crab, whose simple preparation casts the spotlight on the exquisite richness of this crustacean. Even when left raw, as in Chilled Pickled Crab, the flavours are delectable. Much of the seafood, like tiny shrimps, squid and anchovies, are also dried as seasoning bases, which can then be combined with meat or poultry to create distinctively southern combinations of meat and fish. Shellfish are also eaten for symbolic reasons. Prawns, for instance, signify happiness and lobster represents the dragon and nobility.

Fish-stuffed vegetables

This complex dish of aubergines and bitter gourd stuffed with seafood paste and served with a squid and tofu broth is Hakka in origin. It is a very popular street food in Singapore and Malaysia, where there are sizeable Cantonese and Hakka communities, as well as in China.

1 Put the soya beans in a large, heavy pan. Pour in the water. Bring to the boil, then lower the heat and simmer for 45 minutes. Strain the stock into a large, shallow pan. Discard the soya beans, reserving a few for the garnish.

2 Put the cubes of fish into a food processor. Process until finely chopped, then add the cornflour and salt. Process in short bursts for about 15 minutes, adding up to 30ml/2 tbsp water, until the mixture has a slightly springy texture. Scrape into a bowl.

3 Slice the aubergine diagonally into 2cm/¾in thick rounds. Slice the bitter gourd into rounds of similar size, also on the diagonal. This will help to keep the filling in place.

4 Make a deep slit in each aubergine piece three quarters down to make a cavity. Remove the pith and seeds from the bitter gourd pieces. Stuff each piece of vegetable with the fish mixture and smooth on both sides with a butter knife.

5 Slice the reconstituted squid into bitesize pieces. Cut the tofu into bite-size chunks. Bring the soya bean stock to a simmer and crumble in the stock cube. Add the squid, tofu and stuffed vegetables and cook for 10 minutes. Serve in bowls, garnished with the reserved soya beans, and with dips of chilli sauce and hoisin sauce on the side.

Variations For an even richer dish, add fish balls and water convolvulus. For a more substantial dish, add boiled noodles.

Serves 4

75g/3oz/½ cup dried soya beans
1 litre/1¾ pints/4 cups water
300g/11oz skinless, boneless
  fish, cubed
15ml/1 tbsp cornflour
  (cornstarch)
5ml/1 tsp salt
1 whole aubergine (eggplant)
1 whole bitter gourd
1 reconstituted dried squid
250g/9oz pack fresh tofu
1 seafood or fish stock cube
chilli sauce and hoisin sauce,
  to serve

Cook's tip Don't skimp on the processing time for the fish; it needs to be springy, and the longer you process it the springier it becomes.

Per portion Energy 226kcal/951kJ; Protein 31.8g; Carbohydrate 8.4g, of which sugars 2.2g; Fat 7.5g, of which saturates 1g; Cholesterol 119mg; Calcium 381mg; Fibre 4g; Sodium 584mg.

Sweet and sour snapper

Originating in the northern region of Shandong, this dish turns up on most regional menus. Comprising simply a whole deep-fried fish served with a medley of vegetables, it is distinguished by the sauce. This is based on Kao Liang wine vinegar, which is made from sorghum and millet grains.

1 Soak the mushrooms in a bowl of boiling water for 20–30 minutes, until soft. Meanwhile, rinse the fish inside and out, then pat dry with kitchen paper. Make deep cuts diagonally across both sides of the fish. Rub with the salt, rinse again and pat dry. Dust the fish all over with the cornflour.

2 Heat the oil in a wok that is large enough to hold the fish comfortably. Carefully lower the fish into the oil and fry over medium heat for 7–8 minutes, until the skin is crisp and golden brown and the fish is cooked through. Remove it from the wok and drain on kitchen paper. Place the fish on a serving platter with a decent lip to hold the sauce, and keep hot.

3 Drain the mushrooms and slice them thinly, discarding the stems. In a clean wok, heat 30ml/2 tbsp oil and stir-fry the ginger and garlic for 1 minute. Add the spring onions, bamboo shoots and pepper, with the sliced mushrooms. Stir-fry for 2 minutes more.

4 Mix all the sauce ingredients in a bowl. Add to the wok, bring rapidly to the boil and simmer for 1 minute, until the sauce thickens. Pour over the fish and garnish with more chopped spring onions. Serve immediately.

Variations

• *Kao Liang* wine vinegar is recommended for its robust flavour, but if you cannot locate it, any wine vinegar can be used.
• The snapper can be substituted with any firm-fleshed fish, such as cod, grouper or halibut. If you find the sight of a whole fish a little off-putting, use fish fillets.

Serves 4

4 dried Chinese black mushrooms
1 whole snapper or similar fish, about
   800g/1¾lb, cleaned and scaled
15ml/1 tbsp salt
45ml/3 tbsp cornflour (cornstarch)
oil for deep- and shallow-frying
15ml/1 tbsp thinly sliced root ginger
15ml/1 tbsp crushed garlic
1 spring onion, cut into 2.5cm/1in
   lengths, plus extra, to garnish
30ml/2 tbsp thinly sliced
   bamboo shoots
½ red (bell) pepper, thinly sliced

For the sauce
60ml/4 tbsp Kao Liang wine vinegar
15ml/1 tbsp sugar
15ml/1 tbsp light soy sauce
10ml/2 tsp cornflour (cornstarch)
   mixed with 45ml/3 tbsp water
200ml/7fl oz/scant 1 cup water
   or stock

Per portion Energy 332kcal/1389kJ; Protein 25.4g; Carbohydrate 14.2g, of which sugars 1.1g; Fat 19.8g, of which saturates 2.6g; Cholesterol 46mg; Calcium 61mg; Fibre 0.2g; Sodium 884mg.

Steamed fish with sour plums

Shantou restaurants take great pride in steamed fish dishes like this one. The addition of sour plums is a particularly inspired touch, especially when salmon, pomfret or sea bass is used, as the tartness of the plums really cuts the rich oils in the fish and perfectly balances the dish.

1 Rinse the fish inside and out. Dry with kitchen paper. Cut deep slashes on either side of the fish, where the flesh is thickest. Put the fish on a plate that will fit in your steamer. If the fish is too large, cut it in half.

2 Drain the sour plums and put them in a bowl. Mash to a rough purée, using a potato masher or a spoon. Spread the purée over the fish.

3 Dribble the fish sauce over the fish and scatter with the ginger and spring onions. Lay the strips of streaky bacon on top.

4 Put the plate in the steamer. Steam the fish over rapidly boiling water for about 15 minutes or until it is cooked through. Transfer everything to a warm platter, garnish with the coriander and serve immediately.

Serves 4

1 whole fish, about 500g/1¼lb,
  cleaned and scaled
4 canned sour plums
15ml/1 tbsp fish sauce
15ml/1 tbsp finely shredded
  root ginger
2 spring onions (scallions),
  finely shredded
3–4 strips of streaky (fatty) bacon
chopped fresh coriander (cilantro),
  to serve

Per portion Energy 188kcal/791kJ; Protein 20.4g; Carbohydrate 9.3g, of which sugars 9.2g; Fat 8g, of which saturates 2.4g; Cholesterol 45mg; Calcium 51mg; Fibre 1.7g; Sodium 658mg.

Serves 4

1 large carp, about 1kg/2¼lb,
  cleaned and scaled
400ml/14fl oz/1⅔ cups water
15ml/1 tbsp grated fresh root ginger
45ml/3 tbsp dark soy sauce
30ml/2 tbsp sesame oil
5ml/1 tsp sugar
pinch of salt and ground black pepper
4 cloves
15ml/1 tbsp cornflour (cornstarch)
  mixed with 30ml/2 tbsp water
spring onions, to garnish (optional)

Per portion Energy 211kcal/883kJ; Protein 22.2g;
Carbohydrate 5.4g, of which sugars 1.9g; Fat 11.4g,
of which saturates 1.9g; Cholesterol 84mg; Calcium
62mg; Fibre 0g; Sodium 590mg.

Braised carp in ginger sauce

Braising fish in water and aromatics is a cooking method that is typical of both the Fujian school of cooking and the neighbouring province of Guangzhou. The recipe is very easy to make – the fish is simply braised in a tasty stock – but the combination of flavours works extremely well.

1 Rinse the carp inside and out. Pat dry with kitchen paper. Make deep cuts diagonally across both sides of the fish. If the fish is too large for your wok, cut it into two pieces.

2 Pour the water into the wok and add the grated ginger, soy sauce, sesame oil, sugar, salt, pepper and cloves. Bring to the boil.

3 Carefully lower the fish into the liquid. Reduce the heat and braise the fish for 15 minutes or until it is cooked through. Lift the fish out and put it on a serving dish. Keep hot.

4 Stir the cornflour mixture into the liquid remaining in the wok. Bring to the boil and cook, stirring constantly, for 2 minutes or until the sauce thickens. Spoon the sauce over the fish, garnish with spring onions, if using, and serve immediately.

Serves 4

16 large tiger prawns (jumbo shrimp)
45ml/3 tbsp vegetable oil
15ml/1 tbsp chopped garlic
15ml/1 tbsp ground black pepper
10ml/2 tsp salt

Cook's tip To appreciate the flavours at their magnificent best, this dish should always be served piping hot.

Salt and pepper prawns

This is the simplest way of preparing prawns in their shells and Cantonese chefs have the technique down to a fine art. Chefs in Hong Kong are particularly skilled, dexterously employing the flash stir-frying method by which they coax flames to catch in the wok. It is pure theatre.

1 Clean the prawns thoroughly and cut off 1cm/½in from the head end of each. Remove the whiskers. If the prawns are particularly large, use a sharp knife to split each one in half down its length.

2 Heat a dry wok. Add the prawns to the hot pan and flash fry over high heat for 2 minutes or until they turn pink, shivering the wok to keep them on the move at all times. Tip the prawns into a bowl.

3 Add the oil to the wok and heat it. When it is very hot, add the garlic and fry for 1 minute, stirring constantly. Add the prawns, with the pepper and salt and stir rapidly over high heat for 2–3 minutes. Cover the wok with a lid and cook for 1 minute more. Transfer the prawns to a dish and serve immediately.

Per portion Energy 172kcal/717kJ; Protein 20.1g; Carbohydrate 2.7g, of which sugars 2.4g; Fat 9g, of which saturates 1.1g; Cholesterol 219mg; Calcium 97mg; Fibre 0.3g; Sodium 1197mg.

Butterfly prawns

A classic Cantonese restaurant dish, this takes its name from the way each prawn is slit and opened out so that it looks like a butterfly. The prawns are dipped in a very light batter, almost like tempura, and then quickly cooked in very hot oil until golden and crispy.

1 Clean the prawns and shell them, but leave the tails intact. Using a sharp knife, slit each prawn halfway through the back, then spread them flat so that they resemble butterflies.

2 Mix the plain flour and self-raising flour in a bowl. Add the bicarbonate of soda, then the sesame oil and cold water. Stir to make a smooth batter.

3 Heat the oil in a wok or deep-fryer to 190°C/375°F. Dip each prawn in turn in the batter, gently shaking off the excess, and add to the hot oil. Repeat with more prawns, but do not overcrowd the wok or fryer.

4 After 2–3 minutes, when the prawns are golden brown, lift them out and drain on kitchen paper. Keep warm while cooking successive batches. Serve hot, with the chilli and garlic dipping sauce.

Serves 4

16 large prawns (shrimp)
30ml/2 tbsp plain (all-purpose) flour
15ml/1 tbsp self-raising
  (self-rising) flour
pinch of bicarbonate of soda
  (baking soda)
15ml/1 tbsp sesame oil
120ml/4fl oz/½ cup cold water
vegetable oil for deep-frying
chilli and garlic dipping sauce, to serve

Per portion Energy 156kcal/653kJ; Protein 12.5g; Carbohydrate 7.3g, of which sugars 0.5g; Fat 8.8g, of which saturates 1.3g; Cholesterol 157mg; Calcium 64mg; Fibre 0.3g; Sodium 316mg.

Red cooked prawns on the shell

Known as ha loke *in Cantonese, this has become a staple dish in Chinese restaurants throughout South-east Asia. For aesthetic reasons, and to maximize the flavour, the prawns are not shelled, although you can remove the heads without compromising the intrinsic flavour too much.*

1 Clean the prawns and cut off 1cm/½in from the head end of each. Using a sharp knife, slice each prawn in half down its length, leaving the shells on.

2 Heat a wok. Dribble the vegetable oil around the rim so that it flows down to coat the surface. When the oil is hot, add the ginger and garlic. Stir-fry for 30 seconds.

3 Add the onion slices and stir-fry for 2 minutes. Toss the prawns into the wok and stir-fry over high heat for 2–3 minutes or until they have turned pink. Using a slotted spoon, transfer the prawns to a bowl.

4 Pour the tomato sauce and oyster sauce into the wok, add the water and quickly bring to the boil, stirring all the time.

5 Arrange the lettuce leaves on a platter or on individual plates. Divide the prawns among them and spoon the sauce over. Serve immediately.

Serves 4

450g/1lb tiger prawns
  (jumbo shrimp)
30ml/2 tbsp vegetable oil
30ml/2 tbsp chopped root ginger
30ml/2 tbsp chopped garlic
1 large onion, sliced
30ml/2 tbsp tomato sauce (ketchup)
30ml/2 tbsp oyster sauce
100 ml/3½fl oz/scant ½ cup water
whole lettuce leaves, to serve

Per portion Energy 154kcal/643kJ; Protein 11.3g; Carbohydrate 13.4g, of which sugars 10.6g; Fat 6.5g, of which saturates 0.9g; Cholesterol 35mg; Calcium 93mg; Fibre 1.8g; Sodium 934mg.

Serves 4–6

4 fresh mottled crabs or
  any small crabs, about
  100–150g/3¾–5oz each
600ml/1 pint/2½ cups rice
  wine vinegar
6 garlic cloves, crushed
25g/1oz root ginger, peeled
  and crushed
25g/1oz/4 tsp rock salt
4 fresh red chillies (optional)

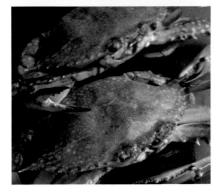

Per portion Energy 45kcal/187kJ; Protein 6.8g;
Carbohydrate 0g, of which sugars 0g; Fat 1.9g, of
which saturates 0.2g; Cholesterol 25mg; Calcium
1mg; Fibre 0g; Sodium 1788mg.

Chilled pickled crab

*Shantou chefs are adept at pickling crustaceans, especially the small
mottled crabs that live on coastal beaches and in tropical mangrove
swamps. When pickled, the crabs keep for weeks in the refrigerator,
and taste very good with plain congee (rice porridge).*

1 Clean the crabs and remove any fibrous matter. Prise the shell away from the body and
cut each crab into four pieces. Trim off the ends of the smaller legs. Remove and discard
any coral. Wash the crabs thoroughly, drain and dry with kitchen paper.

2 Put the vinegar in a non-reactive pan and add the garlic, ginger and salt, together with the
whole chillies, if using. Bring to the boil. Remove the pan of pickling liquid from the heat and
leave until cold.

3 Pack the crabs in one or more sterilized jars and pour over the pickling liquid so that the
crabs are completely submerged. If using more than one jar, divide the chillies among them.

4 Close the jars, making sure they are airtight. Store in the refrigerator, stirring once every
day with a clean dry spoon. The pickled crabs will be ready for eating after the third day.

Serves 4

4 whole crabs, about 250g/9oz each
15ml/1 tbsp chopped root ginger
30ml/2 tbsp Chinese wine
15ml/1 tbsp light soy sauce
5ml/1 tsp ground black pepper
chilli and garlic sauce, for dipping

Wenchang steamed crab

A small county town on the east coast of Hainan Island, Wenchang has two major claims to fame. The first is its excellent seafood, and the second is as the ancestral home of two sisters, Song Qingling and Song Meiling, the wives of Generals Sun Yat Sen and Chiang Kai Shek respectively.

1 Clean the crabs and remove the belly flap from each, together with any fibrous tissue attached to it. Prise the shell away from the body and cut each crab into four pieces. Crack the large claws for easy removal of the meat after the crabs are cooked.

2 Mix the ginger, wine, soy sauce and pepper in a shallow heatproof bowl which will both accommodate all the crabs and fit in your steamer.

3 Put the bowl in the steamer and cook the crabs over boiling water for 15 minutes or until they turn pink all over. Serve hot or cold, with chilli and garlic sauce on the side for dipping.

Variations The liquor that collects at the bottom of the plate or bowl in any steamed shellfish dish is delicious when mixed with rice.

Per portion Energy 119kcal/495kJ; Protein 17.1g; Carbohydrate 0.4g, of which sugars 0.3g; Fat 4.8g, of which saturates 0.5g; Cholesterol 63mg; Calcium 1mg; Fibre 0g; Sodium 642mg.

Scallops with black bean sauce

When scallops are fresh, they taste exquisite when simply steamed in their shells. Here they are served with a little flavoursome sauce made from Chinese wine, black bean sauce and fresh ginger, which perfectly complements the sweet tender flesh of the scallops.

1 Preheat the oven to 160°C/325°F/Gas 3. Spread the scallops in a single layer on a baking sheet. Heat them for a few moments until they gape, then remove them from the oven.

2 Hold a scallop in a clean dish towel, flat side up. Using a long, flexible knife, run the blade along the inner surface of the flat shell to cut through the muscle that holds the shells together. Ease the shells apart completely.

3 Lift off the top shell. Pull out and discard the black intestinal sac and the yellowish frilly membrane. Cut the white scallop and orange coral from the bottom shell and rinse briefly under cold water. Remove and discard the white ligament attached to the scallop flesh.

4 Mix the wine, black beans, ginger and sugar in a shallow dish. Add the scallops and marinate for 30 minutes.

5 Return the scallops and marinade to the half shells and place them in a steamer. If you have bought shelled scallops, divide them – and the marinade – among four ramekins. Steam for 10 minutes. Chop the spring onions and use to garnish the scallops. Serve.

Serves 4

8 scallops, preferably in the shell
30ml/2 tbsp Chinese Hsiao Hsing wine
15ml/1 tbsp fermented black beans
15ml/1 tbsp chopped root ginger
2.5ml/½ tsp sugar
15ml/1 tbsp spring onions (scallions)

Per portion Energy 75kcal/319kJ; Protein 12.3g; Carbohydrate 3.9g, of which sugars 0.9g; Fat 0.8g, of which saturates 0.2g; Cholesterol 24mg; Calcium 19mg; Fibre 0.3g; Sodium 91mg.

Stir-fried squid and mangetout

Like many people who live near the sea, the Cantonese have a passion for all shellfish. Squid and octopus are especially popular, both at home and as premium restaurant dishes. They demand skilful cooking as they rapidly become rubbery and unpalatable if overdone.

1 Using a sharp knife or kitchen scissors, slice through the side of each squid tube and open them out so that they lie flat.

2 Cross-hatch the surface of each piece of squid by making deep cuts at 1cm/½in intervals, first in one direction and then in the other. Cut each piece of squid in half lengthways.

3 Heat the oil in a wok and fry the garlic for 30 seconds. Toss in the mangetout and the pieces of squid and fry over high heat for 2 minutes. Add the oyster sauce, pepper and sesame oil and stir for 1 minute.

4 Mix the cornflour with the water in a small bowl. Add the mixture to the wok and stir until the sauce thickens and bubbles. Spoon into a serving bowl and serve immediately.

Serves 4

175g/6oz squid tubes, cleaned
15ml/1 tbsp vegetable oil
30ml/2 tbsp garlic, crushed
175g/6oz mangetouts
  (snow peas), trimmed
30m/2 tbsp oyster sauce
2.5ml/½ tsp ground
  black pepper
30ml/2 tbsp sesame oil
10ml/2 tsp cornflour (cornstarch)
105ml/7 tbsp water

Per portion Energy 141kcal/589kJ; Protein 8.5g; Carbohydrate 6.8g, of which sugars 3.6g; Fat 9.1g, of which saturates 1.3g; Cholesterol 98mg; Calcium 27mg; Fibre 1.1g; Sodium 173mg.

Serves 4

450g/1lb live green-lipped or
  standard mussels, scrubbed
  and bearded
30ml/2 tbsp vegetable oil
15ml/1 tbsp chopped root ginger
3 garlic cloves, chopped
30ml/2 tbsp Chinese wine
  or sherry
150ml/¼ pint/⅔ cup water
2.5ml/½ tsp salt
2.5ml/½ tsp ground black pepper

Per portion Energy 97kcal/404kJ; Protein 5.7g;
Carbohydrate 2.4g, of which sugars 0.2g; Fat 6.3g,
of which saturates 0.8g; Cholesterol 18mg; Calcium
18mg; Fibre 0.3g; Sodium 355mg.

Stir-fried mussels in ginger sauce

*Any kind of edible bivalve can be used, but green-lipped mussels are ideal
for this dish. Mussels have a great affinity with aromatics like ginger and
garlic and, when steeped in a wine sauce, echo the French dish Moules
Marinière. Hong Kong chefs sometimes use large clams instead.*

1 Carefully check over the mussels, discarding any that have cracked shells, as well as any
that are open and that do not snap shut when tapped on a firm surface.

2 Heat the oil in a wok and fry the ginger and garlic for 40 seconds, until light brown. Add
the mussels and stir rapidly over high heat for 2 minutes, shaking the pan to move the
mussels around.

3 Pour in the Chinese wine or sherry and water. Season with the salt and pepper and
toss the mussels over the heat for a further 2–3 minutes, until all of them have opened.
Discard any mussels that remain closed. Pile the mussels into a warm serving bowl and
serve immediately.

Cook's tip Drizzle a little sesame oil on top of the mussels just before serving for a nutty
fragrance and added flavour.

Poultry

Apart from Peking duck and crispy aromatic duck, poultry is rarely, if ever, prepared and served whole in China. Convection ovens, which westerners take for granted, are not integral to Chinese kitchens, other than in those of affluent urbanites. Instead, the meat is usually cooked and served in juicy bitesize pieces that can be easily eaten with chopsticks. Chinese cooks have a high regard for poultry and will coax maximum flavour out of every bird. Fried, boiled, steamed or roasted, many iconic Chinese poultry dishes like Cantonese Roast Duck are so delicious they have become firm favourites all over the world.

Light bites and family feasts

Chinese cuisine did not evolve on the basis of roasting or baking, as fuel is scarce and expensive. Instead, meat is often stir-fried, steamed, stewed or braised. Even if the bird is cooked whole, as in the Hainan classic Chicken with Ginger Wine, it will arrive at the table expertly carved and jointed. Knives are frowned on as table cutlery, as it is deemed that this is a job for the cook.

However poultry is cooked, there is almost always a marinade. Even the simplest steamed chicken or braised duck dish will have many seasonings and aromatics to help bring out their flavours and cut the fat. Ginger, garlic, spring onions (scallions) and soy sauce make up the classic flavourings, while wine gives a heady lift to gamey dishes like Crispy Quail. Sweet sauces made from fruit like plums are also popular.

The balance of flavours and textures is, as ever, all important, and one star in this regard is Duck Stuffed with Glutinous Rice, with its compendium of fillings, including lotus seeds, ginkgo nuts and mushrooms. Other dishes, such as Chicken with Cashew Nuts from Hong Kong, are simpler, but still display a splendid interplay of flavours and textures.

Chicken with cashew nuts

This classic, must-have restaurant dish has an intriguing, universal appeal, which can perhaps be explained by the pleasing contrast of the succulent chicken and crunchy cashews, and similar interplay between the sweetness of the carrots and the saltiness of the soy sauce.

1 Bring a small pan of water to the boil. Add the cubed carrot. Blanch for 1 minute, then drain and set aside.

2 Heat the oil in a wok and fry the garlic over medium heat until light brown. Do not let it burn or it will taste bitter.

3 Add the chicken cubes and stir-fry for 2 minutes until almost cooked. Add the carrot, with the cashew nuts, light soy sauce and sesame oil. Stir-fry for 1 minute.

4 Put the cornflour in a small bowl and stir in the water to make a paste. Add to the wok and stir over the heat until the sauce simmers and thickens. Spoon the mixture into a heated dish and serve immediately.

Serves 4

1 carrot, about 115g/4oz, cubed
30ml/2 tbsp vegetable oil
2 garlic cloves, crushed
2 boneless chicken breast fillets, skinned and diced
150g/5oz/1¼ cups cashew nuts
15ml/1 tbsp light soy sauce
15ml/1 tbsp sesame oil
5ml/1 tsp cornflour (cornstarch)
150ml/¼ pint/⅔ cup water

Per portion Energy 297kcal/1244kJ; Protein 32g; Carbohydrate 12.5g, of which sugars 9g; Fat 13.6g, of which saturates 2.5g; Cholesterol 79mg; Calcium 51mg; Fibre 2.4g; Sodium 131mg.

Plum sauce chicken

The fruity sweetness of plum sauce is the perfect foil for meat and poultry, either on its own or as an ingredient in a sweet and sour sauce. Here, it partners tender chicken that is coated with cracker crumbs and quickly deep-fried to give a flavoursome and crisp crust.

1 Cut each chicken breast into four pieces. Put the egg in one shallow bowl and the cracker crumbs in another. Heat the oil in a wok or deep-fryer.

2 Dip each piece of chicken in egg and then in cracker crumbs, patting the crumbs on firmly to coat. Discard any excess crumbs.

3 Deep-fry, in batches if necessary, for 3–4 minutes, until golden brown and cooked through. Using a slotted spoon, transfer to a board.

4 Put the plum sauce and hoisin sauce in a pan and stir in the water. Heat until bubbling. Meanwhile cut the chicken into bitesize pieces and pile on a serving platter.

5 Pour the sauce over the chicken, garnish with the cucumber sticks and serve.

Serves 4

2 boneless chicken breast
  fillets, skinned
1 egg, beaten
6 crackers, finely crushed
  (about ⅔ cup cracker crumbs)
vegetable oil for deep-frying
45ml/3 tbsp plum sauce
15ml/1 tbsp hoisin sauce
100ml/3½fl oz/scant ½ cup water
cucumber sticks, to garnish

Per portion Energy 270kcal/1132kJ; Protein 20.4g; Carbohydrate 16g, of which sugars 8.8g; Fat 14.3g, of which saturates 2.4g; Cholesterol 91mg; Calcium 23mg; Fibre 0.3g; Sodium 188mg.

Chicken with shrimp paste

This new dish is an innovation that draws on Singaporean cooking elements in its use of shrimp paste, ground coriander and turmeric. These ingredients are generally unknown in southern Chinese cooking but have been adopted with enthusiasm in recent years as they add an extra savoury note to a simple dish.

1 Rinse the chicken thighs under cold running water then pat dry with kitchen paper. Cut each chicken thigh into 2–3 pieces.

2 Put the shrimp paste in a small bowl and add the water. Mash well to mix, then add the ground coriander and turmeric, with the pepper and sugar. Mix to a smooth paste. Spread out the cornflour in a shallow bowl.

3 Rub the paste all over the chicken, pressing it in well, then transfer the pieces to the bowl of cornflour and coat them on all sides.

4 Heat the vegetable oil in a wok or deep-fryer to 190°C/375°F. Carefully add the coated chicken pieces and deep-fry, in batches if necessary, for 3–4 minutes, until golden brown and cooked through.

5 Lift out the pieces using a slotted spoon and keep hot while you cook the remaining pieces in the same way. Drain on kitchen paper to absorb any excess oil and serve immediately with a chilli dipping sauce.

Variation To give this dish extra fire, add 2.5ml/½ tsp chilli powder to the seasoning.

Serves 4

450g/1lb boneless chicken thighs
20g/¾oz shrimp paste
30ml/2 tbsp water
30ml/2 tbsp ground coriander
5ml/1 tsp ground turmeric
5ml/1 tsp ground black pepper
10ml/2 tsp sugar
115g/4oz/1 cup cornflour
  (cornstarch)
vegetable oil for deep-frying
chilli dipping sauce, to serve

Cook's tip Known as *belacan* in Malay and *ha cheong* in Cantonese, shrimp paste has a sharp pungency that is tempered and subtly muted when cooked.

Per portion Energy 411kcal/1721kJ; Protein 31.5g; Carbohydrate 30g, of which sugars 0g; Fat 19.4g, of which saturates 2.5g; Cholesterol 104mg; Calcium 88mg; Fibre 0g; Sodium 302mg.

Chicken and banana rolls

Bananas do not often turn up in savoury cooking but in Hong Kong and Hainan Island, the fruit has a special place in the kitchen. In this unique dish, sweet chunks of banana are wrapped in succulent chicken and deep-fried, making an unusual but delicious snack.

1 Slice the chicken breasts diagonally into 3–4 thin escalopes. Put these between pieces of clear film (plastic wrap) and pound lightly with a meat mallet to tenderize.

2 Put the beaten egg in one shallow bowl and spread out the cornflour in another.

3 Slice each banana into 3–4 lengths. Dip each piece in a little egg and place on an escalope. Fold up and over to make a secure roll. Coat the roll with cornflour, patting the coating on firmly. Set aside.

4 Heat the vegetable oil in a wok or deep-fryer to 190°C/375°F. Fry the rolls, in batches if necessary, for 3–4 minutes, until crisp and golden brown. Drain on kitchen paper, then slice each chicken and banana roll diagonally, pile the pieces on a plate and serve.

Serves 4

2 boneless chicken breast
  fillets, skinned
1 egg, lightly beaten
150g/5oz/1¼ cups cornflour
  (cornstarch)
2 ripe bananas
vegetable oil for
  deep-frying

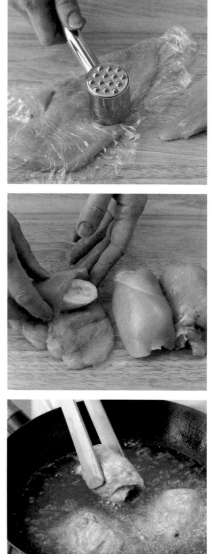

Per portion Energy 402kcal/1689kJ; Protein 20.4g; Carbohydrate 46.1g, of which sugars 10.5g; Fat 16.4g, of which saturates 2.3g; Cholesterol 100mg; Calcium 20mg; Fibre 0.6g; Sodium 83mg.

Chicken with ginger wine

The rub for this recipe isn't based on a Chinese product, but rather on a ginger wine that has been made in England since the 18th century. It is widely available, but gingered Chinese wine or sherry can be used instead. Steaming the chicken makes it very tender, and the ginger gives it a wonderful flavour.

1 Place the chicken on a deep plate that will fit in your wok or steamer. Put the grated ginger in a bowl and add the salt. Stir in the ginger wine, Chinese wine or sherry. Spread the mixture over the chicken and rub it in well.

2 Cut the spring onions into 5cm/2in lengths and then into fine strips. Slit the chillies, remove the seeds and slice the flesh into thin strips. Scatter these evenly over the chicken, with half the spring onion strips.

3 Place the plate containing the chicken in the steamer or wok. Cover and steam for 1 hour or until it is cooked through, topping up the water in the steamer as necessary.

4 Carve the chicken and arrange the pieces on a platter. Serve hot or cold, garnished with the remaining spring onion strips.

Serves 6

1 whole chicken, about 1.6kg/3½lb

30ml/2 tbsp finely grated fresh
   root ginger

5ml/1 tsp salt

60ml/4 tbsp ginger wine, Chinese
   wine or sherry

5 spring onions (scallions)

2 fresh red chillies

Per portion Energy 394kcal/1634kJ; Protein 33g;
Carbohydrate 0.5g, of which sugars 0.4g; Fat 27.6g,
of which saturates 8g; Cholesterol 171mg; Calcium
20mg; Fibre 0.1g; Sodium 136mg.

Soy-braised chicken

The local name for this Cantonese classic is see yau gai *and it has as many variations as a chicken has feathers. Guangzhou Cantonese do not use galangal, but Cantonese in Singapore and Malaysia insist on it. Caramelizing the chicken gives it a delicious bittersweet flavour.*

1 Heat the oil in a wok large enough to hold the chicken. Sprinkle in the sugar and cook over medium to high heat until the mixture froths and caramelizes. When it is pale brown in colour, add the chicken and turn it several times to coat the skin.

2 Add the soy sauce to the wok. Using two spatulas or large forks, turn the chicken several times to coat it thoroughly and let it steep in the sauce.

3 Add the garlic, galangal and water. Bring to the boil, reduce the heat, cover and simmer for 50 minutes. Turn off the heat, leaving the wok covered with the lid, and leave for a further 10 minutes, during which time the chicken will continue to cook.

4 Check that the chicken is fully cooked, then transfer it to a board. Cover with foil and leave to stand. Strain the cooking liquid into a pan. Discard the solids in the strainer.

5 Bring the liquid in the pan to the boil, add the cornflour mixture and stir until the sauce is thick and glossy.

6 Carve the chicken and arrange the slices on a platter. Garnish with the cucumber. Serve the thick, slightly reduced, sauce on the side with a side dip of chilli sauce, if you like.

Variation For a sauce with a more intense garlic flavour, do not throw away the garlic cloves with the knob of galangal after straining. Instead, crush them to a purée and return them to the sauce.

Serves 4–6

30ml/2 tbsp vegetable oil
15ml/1 tbsp sugar
1 chicken, about 1.6kg/3½lb
150ml/¼ pint/⅔ cup dark soy sauce
8 garlic cloves, peeled and bruised
1 large knob of galangal, bruised
1.5 litres/2½ pints/6¼ cups water
30ml/2 tbsp cornflour (cornstarch)
  mixed with 30ml/2 tbsp water
sliced cucumber, to garnish
chilli sauce, to serve (optional)

Cook's tip Galangal is a rhizome, like ginger. There are two types: greater galangal, which comes from Indonesia, while lesser galangal is a native of southern China. The latter, used here, has a pungent flavour, like a cross between ginger and black pepper.

Per portion Energy 445kcal/1846kJ; Protein 33g; Carbohydrate 8.2g, of which sugars 3.5g; Fat 31.2g, of which saturates 8.4g; Cholesterol 171mg; Calcium 18mg; Fibre 0g; Sodium 1026mg.

Jade and silver chicken

The name of this dish stems from the use of broccoli and chicken, which symbolize jade and silver. Pretty, tasty and nutritious, it is a star item in most Chinese restaurants around the world. Traditionally, Chinese kinhua ham is used but this is rarely found outside China and any smoked or honey-cured ham can be used to good effect.

1 Put the chicken breasts in a pan and pour over the water. Bring to the boil, lower the heat and simmer for 10 minutes or until cooked through. Lift out the chicken portions with tongs and put them on a board. Reserve the cooking liquid in the pan.

2 Slice the ham into 2.5cm/1in wide strips and cut the spears of broccoli into strips of similar length. Slice each piece of chicken in half lengthways and then in 2.5cm/1in strips.

3 Layer the broccoli, ham and chicken strips in a deep plate that will fit inside a wok or steamer. Steam the mixture over rapidly boiling water for 5 minutes.

4 Meanwhile, in a small bowl, mix the cornflour to a paste with a little of the water used for cooking the chicken. Crumble the chicken stock cube into the remaining water in the pan and add the cornflour paste, Chinese wine, sesame oil and black pepper. Bring to the boil, stirring, until the sauce has the consistency of pouring cream.

5 Remove the steamed broccoli, ham and chicken from the steamer and pour the sauce over the top. Serve immediately.

Variation Use prosciutto or Chinese ham instead of the honey-cured or smoked ham.

Serves 4

2 boneless chicken breast fillets, skin on
250ml/8fl oz/1 cup water
2 slices honey-cured or smoked ham
150g/5oz Chinese broccoli (kai lan) or tenderstem broccoli
15ml/1 tbsp cornflour (cornstarch)
½ chicken stock cube
30ml/2 tbsp Chinese wine
30ml/2 tbsp sesame oil
5ml/1 tsp ground black pepper

Cook's tip Tenderstem broccoli is rich in nutrients. It is aptly named as the stalks or stems have a texture that resembles asparagus. It is available in many supermarkets.

Per portion Energy 182kcal/763kJ; Protein 22.9g; Carbohydrate 4.4g, of which sugars 0.9g; Fat 7.3g, of which saturates 1.3g; Cholesterol 63mg; Calcium 28mg; Fibre 1g; Sodium 261mg.

Hainan chicken rice

This dish originated from Hainan Island, where it evolved into a classic street food but has now been elevated to five-star status in hotels and upmarket restaurants. Comprising tender chunks of poached chicken mixed with rice and aromatics, it is always served with a classic quartet of dips – dark soy sauce, finely chopped fresh chilli, finely chopped fresh root ginger and finely chopped garlic – with a bowl of soup on the side.

1 Trim off and discard any excess fat from the chicken, then place it in a large pan. Pour in the water. It should just cover the chicken, so top up if necessary.

2 Add the onion, garlic, peppercorns, ginger, soy sauce and sesame oil to the pan. Bring to the boil, lower the heat and simmer, uncovered, for 40 minutes. Turn off the heat, cover and leave to stand for about 15 minutes, during which time it will continue to cook by means of residual heat.

3 Check that the chicken is fully cooked. Lift it out of the stock, put it on a platter and keep it hot. Strain the stock into a clean pan.

4 Put the rice in a colander and rinse it well. Drain, then tip into a pan. Add enough of the chicken stock to cover the rice by 2.5cm/1in. Bring to the boil, cover the pan and reduce the heat to medium. Cook for 15 minutes.

5 Meanwhile, heat the stock remaining in the pan. Taste and adjust the seasoning. When the rice is dry and fluffy, spoon it into a heated bowl. Put the soup in a separate bowl and garnish it with the chopped spring onions.

6 Cut up the chicken and arrange it on a large platter. Garnish with the slices of cucumber and tomato. Mix together the finely chopped chilli and the vinegar to make a sour sauce. Serve the chicken with the rice, the soup, and small side dishes of chilli and vinegar sauce, garlic, ginger and soy sauce.

Serves 4

1 chicken, about 1.6kg/3½lb
1.2 litres/2 pints/5 cups water
½ large onion, sliced
4 garlic cloves, peeled and left whole
10 black peppercorns
1 large knob of fresh root
   ginger, bruised
15ml/1 tbsp soy sauce
30ml/2 tbsp sesame oil
200g/7oz/1 cup long grain white
   rice or jasmine rice
chopped spring onions (scallions),
   to garnish the soup
sliced cucumber and tomatoes,
   to garnish

To serve
30ml/2 tbsp chilli
60ml/4 tbsp vinegar
30ml/2 tbsp finely chopped garlic
30ml/2 tbsp finely chopped fresh
   root ginger
30ml/2 tbsp dark soy sauce

Per portion Energy 802kcal/3333kJ; Protein 52.7g; Carbohydrate 41.1g, of which sugars 0.9g; Fat 47g, of which saturates 12.8g; Cholesterol 256mg; Calcium 34mg; Fibre 0.2g; Sodium 201mg.

Duck stuffed with glutinous rice

if you have a helpful butcher, ask him to debone the duck for you. Otherwise, stuff it on the bone. This version has similarities with the classic Shanghai recipe called Eight Treasure Duck but has been tweaked to suit Cantonese tastes. Start preparations the day before serving.

1 Rinse the glutinous rice in several changes of cold water, then leave it to soak overnight in a bowl of fresh cold water. Next day, drain the rice and spread it evenly in a steamer lined with cheesecloth. Cover and steam over simmering water for 25 minutes or until tender and fluffy.

2 Meanwhile, soak the mushrooms in boiling water for 20–30 minutes, until soft. Drain, remove the hard stalks and dice the caps finely. Put the mushrooms in a bowl and add the rice, dates, ginkgo nuts, pepper and oyster sauce. Mix well.

3 Remove the excess fat from the duck and enlarge the entrance to the cavity slightly. Stuff it with the rice mixture. Using a poultry needle and fairly strong thread, sew up the slit. Rub the duck all over with half the soy sauce.

4 Heat the oil in a large wok and add the duck. Fry, turning frequently, until the skin is well sealed and brown. Place the duck in a deep pan. Pour in the water and add the sesame oil, spring onions, garlic cloves, remaining soy sauce and black pepper. Bring to the boil. Cover, lower the heat and simmer for 2–2¼ hours, turning several times and topping up the water when necessary.

5 When the duck is cooked, lift it on to a platter. Carve it in the kitchen or serve it at the table, to be carved with a flourish.

Cook's tip Don't waste the stock used for cooking the duck. Strain it into a clean pan and boil it for 30 minutes until it has reduced. Pour into a jug (pitcher), cool quickly, then chill in the refrigerator until the fat solidifies on the top and can be removed and discarded. The stock can be heated and served as a sauce or tossed with stir-fried noodles.

Serves 6–8

75g/3oz/½ cup raw glutinous rice
6 dried black Chinese mushrooms
6 Chinese sweet red dates or
 Medjool dates, pitted and chopped
20 canned ginkgo nuts, drained
2.5ml/½ tsp ground black pepper
45ml/3 tbsp oyster sauce
1 oven-ready duck, about
 2.5kg/5½lb
60ml/4 tbsp dark soy sauce
150ml/¼ pint/⅔ cup oil
2 litres/3½ pints/8 cups water
30ml/2 tbsp sesame oil
2 spring onions (scallions)
6 garlic cloves, peeled and
 left whole
2.5ml/½ tsp ground black pepper

Variation Chinese sweet red dates are called *mat cho*. Look for them in Chinese food stores, or use Medjools or other Middle-Eastern dates instead.

Per portion Energy 504kcal/2092kJ; Protein 21.7g; Carbohydrate 14.1g, of which sugars 6.3g; Fat 40.3g, of which saturates 7.9g; Cholesterol 119mg; Calcium 28mg; Fibre 1.3g; Sodium 755mg.

Cantonese roast duck

You see this vermilion-coloured bird hanging in every Chinese restaurant window, usually with the head still on. There is a reason for this: Chinese-Taoist belief holds that no living creature should go into the afterlife with parts missing. Few take this superstition seriously, but the tradition persists simply because there is a lot of flavour in the head and neck.

1 Clean the duck inside and out and pat it dry with kitchen paper. Tie kitchen string (twine) firmly around the legs of the bird and suspend it from a butcher's hook from a shelf in the kitchen or garage, whichever is the coolest. Place a bowl underneath to catch the drips and leave to dry overnight.

2 Next day, bring a large pan of water to the boil. Add the duck and blanch it for 3–4 minutes. This will remove excess fat and also shrink the skin, promoting crispness when cooked. Lift the duck out of the pan, drain it thoroughly and dry it well with kitchen paper.

3 Put the maltose or honey in a bowl and stir in the hoisin sauce and wine, with the colouring, if using. Generously brush the mixture all over the duck skin. Leave to dry for 1–1½ hours.

4 Preheat the oven to the highest setting: 240–250°C/475–500°F/Gas 9–10. Put the duck on a rack over a roasting pan and roast in the oven for 20 minutes.

5 Reduce the oven temperature to 200°C/400°F/Gas 6 and roast for 30 minutes. Remove the duck from the oven and pierce the thickest part of the thigh with a sharp knife. If the juice runs out clear, turn off the oven, return the duck to it and leave it to continue cooking in residual heat for another 20 minutes. If the duck juices are still a little bloody, leave the oven on and check the bird again after 10–15 minutes.

6 Let the duck cool a little, then chop it up or slice it off the bone into serving pieces. Pile on a platter and serve with sliced cucumber and a chilli sauce for dipping.

Serves 8

1 duck, about 2.5kg/5½lb
15ml1 tbsp maltose or honey
15ml/1 tbsp hoisin sauce
30ml/2 tbsp Chinese wine
15ml/1 tbsp red cochineal food
   colouring (optional)
sliced cucumber and chilli sauce,
   to serve

Cook's tip If you take the duck off the bone for serving, use the bones to make a flavoursome stock. To make, sauté 1 chopped onion, 2 chopped celery stalks and 1 chopped carrot in 15ml/1 tbsp vegetable oil for 5 minutes, until softened slightly. Add the bones and enough water to cover. Add a bay leaf and a few black peppercorns, cover and bring to a simmer. Simmer for about an hour, then strain the liquid into a clean pan. Bring to the boil and reduce by half. Cool quickly and skim off any fat.

Per portion Energy 306kcal/1274kJ; Protein 20.8g; Carbohydrate 1.5g, of which sugars 1.5g; Fat 23.7g, of which saturates 7g; Cholesterol 144mg; Calcium 13mg; Fibre 0g; Sodium 116mg.

30ml/2 tbsp vegetable oil
30ml/2 tbsp sugar
1 oven-ready duck, about
  2.5kg/5½lb
150ml/¼ pint/⅔ cup dark soy sauce
1 large knob galangal or fresh
  root ginger
6 garlic cloves, peeled and bruised
4 star anise
5cm/2in piece of cinnamon stick
2 litres/3½ pints/8 cups water
sliced cucumber, to garnish

Soy-braised duck

A traditional Cantonese dish, this takes time to prepare but is well worth the effort. The method is similar to that for Soy-braised Chicken apart from the addition of star anise and cinnamon and the longer cooking time. It is served – usually cold – for festive occasions, washed down with brandy.

1 Heat the oil in a wok large enough to hold the duck. Sprinkle in the sugar and cook over medium to high heat until the mixture froths and caramelizes. When it is pale brown in colour, add the duck and turn it several times to coat the skin.

2 Add the soy sauce to the wok. Using two spatulas or large forks, turn the duck several times to coat it thoroughly.

3 Add the galangal or ginger, with the garlic cloves, star anise and cinnamon. Pour in the water and bring to the boil. Lower the heat, cover the wok and simmer the duck for 1½ hours or until it is tender and the meat starts to come off the bones.

4 Lift the duck on to a board and set it aside while you make the gravy. Strain the cooking liquid into a clean pan, skim the surplus fat from the surface and boil over high heat until reduced to the consistency of gravy. Carve the duck and arrange on a platter. Garnish with cucumber slices and serve with the gravy.

Per portion Energy 119kcal/498kJ; Protein 10.2g; Carbohydrate 4.6g, of which sugars 3.4g; Fat 6.9g, of which saturates 1.5g; Cholesterol 50mg; Calcium 35mg; Fibre 1.1g; Sodium 412mg.

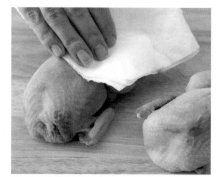

Crispy quail

Quail is not as popular as some other types of poultry, but when you can get them, these birds make delicious eating. Supermarkets usually sell quail in packs of two or four as each bird is very small. Cook two per person as an appetizer. To serve this dish as a main course, double the quantities.

1 Rinse the quail inside and out and pat them dry thoroughly with kitchen paper. The drier the skin before cooking, the crispier it will be after cooking.

2 Mix the salt, five-spice powder and wine in a small bowl. Rub the quail all over with the mixture. Set aside for 30 minutes.

3 Heat the vegetable oil in a wok or deep-fryer to 190ºC/375ºF. Add the quail, in batches if necessary, and deep-fry for 4–6 minutes, turning once or twice, until crisp and golden brown. Lift out and drain on kitchen paper.

4 Put the quail on a serving platter or individual plates and serve hot, with the lemon wedges for squeezing over the crispy skin.

Serves 2

4 quail
5ml/1 tsp salt
2.5ml/½ tsp five-spice powder
30ml/2 tbsp Chinese wine
vegetable oil for deep frying
lemon wedges, to serve

Variation Five-spice powder is a pungent spice, so use it judiciously. It isn't to everyone's taste, so if you do not like it, use 5ml/1 tsp ground coriander instead.

Per portion Energy 462kcal/1938kJ; Protein 77.1g; Carbohydrate 0.2g, of which sugars 0.2g; Fat 15.1g, of which saturates 3.9g; Cholesterol 0mg; Calcium 99mg; Fibre 0g; Sodium 212mg.

Meat

Although all kinds of meat are eaten in China, the favoured animal protein is pork. In Cantonese cooking especially, it rules the culinary realm, turning up in a hundred different guises. The dish it is intended for dictates the way pork is cut, rather than the cut of meat determining what dish is cooked, as occurs in the western world. Whatever animal is eaten, the southern Chinese make good use of every part, from the kidneys and innards to the ribs, combining them with carefully selected ingredients and cooking techniques in a manner that will maximize the flavour.

Sticky snacks and flavour fusions

Meat, especially pork, is very popular in south China, and there is a huge range of dishes that employ it. These follow the principle that a dish should contain a specific ratio of lean meat to fat to skin.

Among the many favourite rib dishes are Spare Ribs in Black Bean Sauce, unctuous in their meatiness, and Cantonese Roast Pork, made from a rib cut that is streaked with fat and cut as a long strip. Marinated in a rich blend of honey, hoisin sauce and preserved red bean curd, it has won legions of fans around the world. Minced pork makes an appearance in dishes like Minced Pork Rolls in Beancurd Skin and all manner of dumplings. When pork is needed for slow-cooking, the hock or leg cut or belly meat is usually used, as in Mist of Harmony.

Offal (variety meats) like liver and kidney are treated with much respect and are manifest in many dishes, which use seasonings to temper their intense flavours. Beef is regarded as a luxury meat and is inevitably imported since there is a very small cattle industry in China. Expensive and hard to come by, it is generally served in restaurant specials like Sautéed Beef in Oyster Sauce, a signature Hong Kong dish.

Serves 4

500g/1¼lb pork spare ribs,
  cut into 5cm/2in lengths

For the marinade
30ml/2 tbsp light soy sauce
5ml/1 tsp sugar
30ml/2 tbsp black bean sauce
30ml/2 tbsp Chinese wine
30ml/2 tbsp oyster sauce
30ml/2 tbsp hoisin sauce
750ml/1¼ pints/3 cups water
spring onions (scallions), to garnish

Spare ribs in black bean sauce

Spare ribs are popular throughout China. Recipes from the south tend to be less rich than those from the north, where marinades contain considerably more wine. The best way to ensure the ribs are really succulent is to braise them, as deep-fried ribs tend to be dry.

1 Combine all the ingredients for the marinade in a large shallow dish. Add the ribs, making sure they are completely submerged. Cover and marinate for 30 minutes, turning the ribs once or twice.

2 Transfer the ribs, with the marinade, to a deep pan. Cover with a tight-fitting lid and bring to the boil. Cook over high heat for 15 minutes.

3 Lower the heat to medium and continue to cook the ribs for a further 40 minutes, until the pork is fully cooked and the sauce is very thick and glossy.

4 Pile the ribs on to a platter, pour the sauce over, garnish with spring onions and serve. The best way to eat ribs is with the fingers, so be sure to have wipes handy.

Per portion Energy 722kcal/3012kJ; Protein 61.8g; Carbohydrate 2.6g, of which sugars 1g; Fat 51.9g, of which saturates 18.1g; Cholesterol 215mg; Calcium 59mg; Fibre 0.7g; Sodium 897mg.

Pork in preserved bean curd

Cantonese chefs use two main types of preserved bean curd: the more common white variety known as fu yee *in Cantonese, and a red one, known as* lam yee. *The latter not only has a more intense flavour, but it also gives the dish a very attractive bright red colour.*

1 With a sharp knife, cut the pork into thin slices. Put the cornflour in a bowl or strong plastic bag, add the pork and toss lightly to coat.

2 Slice the onion and garlic finely. Heat the oil in a wok and fry the onion for 2 minutes. Add the garlic and fry for 1 minute.

3 Push the onion and garlic to the sides of the wok and add the pork slices to the centre. Stir-fry for 2–3 minutes, until the pork is well sealed. Bring the onion mixture back to the centre and mix it with the pork.

4 Add the preserved red bean curd and mash well with your ladle or a fork. Continue to stir-fry the mixture until the pork is thoroughly coated in the beancurd mixture.

5 Add the sugar and water and bring to a brisk boil. When the sauce has reduced to about half the volume, the pork should be done. Serve hot with rice or noodles.

Serves 4

450g/1lb pork rib-eye steak
  streaked with a little fat
15ml/1 tbsp cornflour (cornstarch)
½ large onion
2 garlic cloves
30ml/2 tbsp oil
30ml/2 tbsp preserved red
  bean curd
5ml/1 tsp sugar
120ml/4 fl oz/½ cup water

Per portion Energy 215kcal/898kJ; Protein 24.9g; Carbohydrate 5.7g, of which sugars 1.9g; Fat 10.4g, of which saturates 2.3g; Cholesterol 71mg; Calcium 51mg; Fibre 0.2g; Sodium 82mg.

Stir-fried pork with ginger

Pork marries well with ginger, garlic and spring onions – three ingredients that are regarded as the essential basis of Chinese seasoning. This is a good Cantonese stand-by for those occasions when you fancy a simple meal. Be lavish with the ginger as it is the hallmark of this dish.

1 Using a sharp knife, cut the pork into thin strips. Place these on a board and tenderize them slightly, using a meat mallet or the blunt edge of a cleaver. Rub the strips with sesame oil and set them aside for 15 minutes.

2 Heat the vegetable oil in a wok. Add the sliced garlic and ginger and fry for 1 minute, until pale brown. Do not let the garlic burn or it will taste bitter.

3 Add the pork strips and spring onions. Stir-fry for 2 minutes, then add the oyster sauce and black pepper. Stir over the heat for 2 minutes until the seasonings have been thoroughly absorbed by the pork.

4 Pour in the wine and water. Continue to cook, stirring, for 2 minutes, until the liquid bubbles and the pork is fully cooked. Spoon into a heated bowl and serve.

Serves 4

250g/9oz pork rib-eye steak
30ml/2 tbsp sesame oil
30ml/2 tbsp vegetable oil
15ml/1 tbsp sliced garlic
40g/1½ oz fresh young root ginger,
  sliced into very fine strips
2 spring onions (scallions)
30ml/2 tbsp oyster sauce
5–10ml/1–2 tsp ground
  black pepper
30ml/2 tbsp Chinese rice wine
30ml/2 tbsp water

Per portion Energy 179kcal/747kJ; Protein 25.3g; Carbohydrate 2.8g, of which sugars 2.1g; Fat 7.4g, of which saturates 1.9g; Cholesterol 71mg; Calcium 21mg; Fibre 0.7g; Sodium 614mg.

Serves 4

300g/11oz leg of pork
1 egg, beaten
75g/3oz/¾ cup cornflour (cornstarch)
oil for deep-frying
1 small carrot, cubed
1 large onion, quartered
1 tomato, quartered
30ml/2 tbsp plum sauce
30ml/2 tbsp hoisin sauce
45ml/3 tbsp pineapple juice or
  15ml/1 tbsp vinegar
200ml/7fl oz/scant 1 cup water

Per portion Energy 727kcal/3035kJ; Protein 32.7g;
Carbohydrate 76.5g, of which sugars 39.4g; Fat
32.8g, of which saturates 5.8g; Cholesterol 272mg;
Calcium 85mg; Fibre 2.7g; Sodium 1048mg.

Sweet and sour pork

The sweet and sour flavours of this iconic dish reflect the yin-yang principle of universal harmony that is at the heart of Chinese cooking. Although it originated in Shanghai, every province has its own version. The sweetening agent is plum sauce and the sourness comes from vinegar or pineapple juice.

1 Cut the pork into 1cm/½in cubes. Have ready a shallow dish containing the beaten egg, and a clean, strong plastic bag, in which the cornflour has been placed. Dip the cubes in the egg, then add them to the bag. Shake well to coat them in the cornflour.

2 Heat the oil in a wok to 190°C/375°F. Fry the coated pork cubes, in batches if necessary, until cooked through and golden brown all over. Lift out and drain on kitchen paper.

3 Carefully drain off all but 15ml/1 tbsp of the oil from the wok. Add the carrot cubes to the oil in the wok and fry for 2 minutes. Add the onion and tomato and stir-fry for 1 minute.

4 In a bowl, mix the plum sauce and hoisin sauce with the pineapple juice or vinegar. Stir in the water. Add to the wok and cook, stirring, for 1 minute. Add the cubes of fried pork to the wok and stir quickly until the ingredients are thoroughly mixed. Serve immediately.

Variation Ring the changes further by adding a few drained canned lychees or half a dozen drained canned or fresh pineapple chunks to the sauce.

Serves 8

900g/2lb pork rib-eye steak,
  in one piece
30ml/2 tbsp honey
  or maltose
30ml/2 tbsp hoisin sauce
15ml/1 tbsp preserved red
  bean curd
30ml/2 tbsp Chinese wine
sliced cucumber and a hot
  chilli sauce dip, to serve

Cantonese roast pork

This classic is based on a pork rib cut that is a mixture of fat and lean meat. Traditionally, chefs use a special clay oven inside which the pork is hung on a metal hook. However, a convection oven will work if you use a rack set in a roasting tin. Some restaurants add red food colouring to the marinade, but this is unnecessary as the hoisin sauce and bean curd provide plenty of colour.

1 If the piece of steak is 7.5cm/3in thick or more, cut it in half horizontally. Using a sharp knife, score the surface at regular intervals to a depth of about 1cm/½in.

2 In a shallow dish that is large enough to allow the piece or pieces of meat to lie flat, mix the honey or maltose with the hoisin. Add the preserved red bean curd, mashing it so that it combines with the other ingredients. Stir in the wine.

3 Add the pork and rub it all over with the marinade, making sure to penetrate the scored cuts. Cover the dish and marinate the pork for 1 hour or overnight.

4 Preheat the oven to 220°C/425°F/Gas 7. Place the piece or pieces of pork on a rack set in a roasting pan. Roast the pork for 20 minutes, then reduce the oven temperature to 180°C/350°F/Gas 4 and roast for 20 minutes more.

5 Preheat the grill (broiler). Place the pan containing the pork under the heat until the surface chars lightly in places. Let the pork cool. Serve in slices, with sliced cucumber and a hot chilli sauce dip.

Per portion Energy 158kcal/664kJ; Protein 24.3g; Carbohydrate 4g, of which sugars 4g; Fat 4.6g, of which saturates 1.6g; Cholesterol 71mg; Calcium 18mg; Fibre 0g; Sodium 141mg.

Mist of harmony

This charming name describes a classic Shantou-style dish consisting of braised pork in soy sauce. Rice is the usual accompaniment, although the northern Chinese have a version that is served with steamed breads. The dark soy sauce specified here is a very thick variety, usually available in Chinese stores. It has a sweet edge to it that serves the dish well.

1 Heat the oil in a wok large enough to hold the piece of pork. Sprinkle in the sugar and cook over medium to high heat until the mixture froths and caramelizes. When it is golden brown in colour, add the pork and turn it on all sides so that it is coated all over with caramel.

2 Add the soy sauce, five-spice powder, water and ginger to the wok. Braise the pork over medium heat for 1 hour or until the pork is tender and the sauce is thick. If the liquid seems to be evaporating too rapidly, lower the heat and cover the wok, or add more water (*see* Cook's tip). Lift the pork on to a plate and set aside to cool.

3 Slice the pork and arrange on a platter, with the cucumber or pickled ginger. Remove the ginger from the sauce in the wok, reheat it, then transfer it to a bowl. Serve with the pork.

Cook's tip With any long-braised dish, it may be necessary to top up the liquid. Make sure any water added is boiling or fairly hot. After adding, check the flavour of the sauce and add more soy sauce if necessary.

Serves 6

30ml/2 tbsp oil
15ml/1 tbsp sugar
900g/2lb belly pork, in one piece
60ml/4 tbsp dark soy sauce
15ml/1 tbsp five-spice powder
1 litre/1¾ pints/4 cups water
2 thumb-size knobs of fresh root
  ginger, bruised
sliced cucumber or pickled ginger,
  to serve

Per portion Energy 551kcal/2276kJ; Protein 20.4g; Carbohydrate 2.6g, of which sugars 2.6g; Fat 51g, of which saturates 17.9g; Cholesterol 96mg; Calcium 12mg; Fibre 0g; Sodium 98mg.

Minced pork rolls in beancurd skin

This classic dish of the Swatow people from Shantou is so sublime that it is often cooked as a festive offering during Taoist festivals. It is nothing like the ubiquitous spring roll and is unique in that it uses crinkly beancurd skins as wrappers. The filling is a rich amalgam of ingredients with delightful, contrasting textures. Unlike many regional Chinese dishes, this is a local dish and seldom appears on menus elsewhere.

1 Put the pork in a bowl and add the shredded carrot. Stir in the soy sauce, black pepper, water chestnuts and spring onions.

2 Lightly beat the egg in a small bowl and add it to the mixture. Stir to combine, then stir in the cornflour and mix well.

3 Bring a small pan of water to the boil. Pinch off a small lump of the pork mixture, add it to the water and boil for 2 minutes. Scoop it out, let it cool slightly, then taste and adjust the seasoning if necessary.

4 Keeping the remaining beancurd sheets covered under a damp dish towel, place one sheet on a flat surface. Spread about 30ml/2 tbsp of the pork mixture along one edge. Roll over one and a half times, fold in the sides, then roll again to make a firm roll. Cut through the bean curd to separate the roll from the sheet. Repeat the action, using more sheets when required, until all the filling has been used

5 Heat the oil in a wok or deep-fryer to 190ºC/375ºF. Add the rolls and fry for 3–4 minutes until golden brown and crisp. Drain on kitchen paper and leave to cool. Slice into diagonal pieces and serve with sliced cucumber and a chilli dipping sauce.

Serves 4

400g/14oz/1¾ cups minced
  (ground) pork
1 small carrot, thinly shredded
10ml/2 tsp light soy sauce
5m/1 tsp ground black pepper
50g/2oz/⅓ cup finely chopped
  drained canned water chestnuts
8 spring onions (scallions),
  finely chopped
1 egg
25g/1oz/¼ cup cornflour (cornstarch)
1 package beancurd skins
vegetable oil for deep-frying
sliced cucumber and chilli
  dipping sauce, to serve

Cook's tip Beancurd skins are sometimes brittle, so wipe each sheet with a damp towel before use.

Per portion Energy 387kcal/1608kJ; Protein 23.8g; Carbohydrate 8.6g, of which sugars 2.4g; Fat 28.9g, of which saturates 6.1g; Cholesterol 114mg; Calcium 158mg; Fibre 0.9g; Sodium 361mg.

Stewed mutton with beancurd sticks

Dry beancurd sticks, called fu choke *in Cantonese, are pale yellow in colour. They have rather a bland taste, but are rich in protein and are believed by the Chinese to be very cooling. They are the perfect foil for rich meats like mutton and lamb. This slow-cooked mutton dish is typical of Hainan cooking and is very robust in flavour, making it an ideal dish for keeping out the cold in the winter months.*

1 Soak the beancurd sticks in a bowl of hot water for about 30 minutes, until soft.

2 Meanwhile, using a sharp knife, cut the mutton or lamb into bitesize chunks. Place them on a board and tenderize them slightly, using a meat mallet or the blunt edge of a cleaver.

3 Heat the oil in a wok and fry the garlic until golden brown. Add the meat and fry for 2 minutes to seal in the flavour.

4 Sprinkle the sugar over the meat, then stir in the dark soy sauce, five-spice powder, water and pepper. Transfer the mixture to a pan, cover with a tight-fitting lid and cook over medium heat for 30 minutes.

5 Drain the beancurd sticks and cut them into 5cm/2in lengths. Stir them into the stew, then replace the lid and simmer for 20 minutes more.

6 Remove the lid, increase the heat to high and cook the stew for a further 10 minutes to drive off any excess liquid and reduce the sauce. Spoon the stew into a heated dish and serve immediately.

Serves 4

100g/3¼oz beancurd sticks
350g/12oz lean mutton
  or lamb
15ml/1 tbsp oil
3 garlic cloves, sliced
5ml/1 tsp sugar
45ml/3 tbsp dark soy sauce
pinch of five-spice powder
600ml/1 pint/2½ cups water
2.5ml/½ tsp ground
  black pepper

Cook's tip If the stew is too oily for your taste, cool it quickly, then put it in the refrigerator. On chilling, the fat will solidify on top and can easily be lifted off. Reheat the stew to serve.

Per portion Energy 209kcal/870kJ; Protein 19.5g; Carbohydrate 2.2g, of which sugars 2g; Fat 13.6g, of which saturates 5g; Cholesterol 67mg; Calcium 137mg; Fibre 0g; Sodium 877mg.

Cantonese beefsteak

This is a typical Hong Kong restaurant dish, which echoes western-style steak but which is cooked by the traditional Cantonese stir-fried method. The unusual ingredient here is Worcestershire sauce, very likely a British colonial touch. This imparts a subtle vinegar and pepper flavour to the dish.

1 Slice the sirloin or rump steak thinly into medallions. Put the cornflour in a bowl or strong plastic bag. Add the steak and toss to coat.

2 In a small bowl, mix the wine or sherry, Worcestershire sauce and oyster sauce. Stir, then set aside.

3 Heat the oil in a wok or frying pan. Add the grated ginger and fry for 30 seconds. Add the beef. Stir-fry over high heat for 1 minute, then pour in the wine and sauce mixture. Stir-fry for 1 minute more, then sprinkle over the sugar.

4 Continue to stir for 2 minutes more for medium-rare, or 3 minutes for well-done beef. Serve on a bed of lettuce leaves.

Serves 4

600g/1lb 6oz sirloin or
  rump (round) steak
15ml/1 tbsp cornflour
  (cornstarch)
30ml/2 tbsp Chinese Mui Kwai Lo
  wine or sweet sherry
15ml/1 tbsp Worcestershire sauce
30ml/2 tbsp oyster sauce
45ml/3 tbsp oil
15ml/1 tbsp grated root ginger
2.5ml/½ tsp sugar
lettuce leaves, to serve

Per portion Energy 365kcal/1518kJ; Protein 34.2g; Carbohydrate 5g, of which sugars 1.5g; Fat 22.2g, of which saturates 6.7g; Cholesterol 87mg; Calcium 17mg; Fibre 0g; Sodium 322mg.

Serves 4

450g/1lb sirloin steak
1 large green (bell) pepper
5ml/1 tsp bicarbonate of soda
  (baking soda)
30ml/2 tbsp oil
2 garlic cloves, crushed
15ml/1 tbsp grated fresh
  root ginger
30ml/2 tbsp oyster sauce
5ml/1 tsp ground black pepper
30ml/2 tbsp cornflour (cornstarch)
  mixed with 45ml/3 tbsp water

Per portion Energy 160kcal/669kJ; Protein 17.5g;
Carbohydrate 2.9g, of which sugars 2.7g; Fat 8.8g, of
which saturates 2g; Cholesterol 44mg; Calcium
10mg; Fibre 0.6g; Sodium 485mg.

Sautéed beef in oyster sauce

Featured on Chinese restaurant menus the world over, this southern dish is one of the easiest to recreate at home. Bicarbonate of soda helps to tenderize beef without altering its flavour. It is important to cut both meat and peppers to the same size so that they cook in the same time.

1 Using a sharp knife or cleaver, cut the steak into thin strips. Cut the green pepper into strips of similar width and length. Put the pepper strips in a bowl and set them aside.

2 Put the bicarbonate of soda into a shallow dish, moisten it with a little water, then add the beef strips. Using clean hands, rub the bicarbonate into the meat. Cover and set aside for 10 minutes.

3 Heat the oil in a wok and fry the garlic and ginger for 40 seconds, until light brown. Drain the beef strips, add them to the wok and stir-fry for 1 minute over high heat. Add the green pepper strips and stir-fry for 1 minute.

4 Stir in the oyster sauce and black pepper, then the cornflour mixture. Continue to stir-fry over high heat for 2 minutes until the meat is well-done. Spoon into a heated bowl and serve immediately.

Serves 4

350g/12oz sirloin or
  rump (round) steak
5ml/1 tsp bicarbonate of soda
  (baking soda)
10g/¼oz dried tangerine
  peel
15ml/1 tbsp vegetable oil
2 garlic cloves, crushed
30ml/2 tbsp sesame oil
5ml/1 tsp sugar
8 spring onions (scallions),
  cut in 5cm/2in pieces
30ml/2 tbsp water

Tangerine peel beef

The tangerine, like the orange, is a fruit with auspicious meaning. The Cantonese name for tangerine, kum, *sounds like the word for gold, which symbolizes prosperity. It is one of the most widely used flavourings and is particularly popular in Cantonese and Sichuan cooking.*

1 Slice the steak into thin strips. Put the bicarbonate of soda into a shallow dish, moisten it with a little water, then add the beef strips. Using clean hands, rub the bicarbonate of soda into the meat. Cover and set aside for 10 minutes.

2 Meanwhile, soak the tangerine peel in a bowl of water. When it is soft, drain it and slice it into thin strips.

3 Heat the oil in a wok and fry the garlic for 40 seconds, until light brown. Do not let it burn. Add the beef. Stir-fry over high heat for 1 minute, then stir in the tangerine peel.

4 Add the sesame oil, sugar, spring onions and water. Stir-fry for 2 minutes or until the beef is cooked the way you like it. Spoon into a dish or individual bowls and serve.

Variation Thin strips of orange, lemon or lime peel can be used instead of tangerine. When paring the fruit, take care to remove only the coloured skin and not the bitter pith underneath. Dry the peel by placing it on sheets of kitchen paper and leaving it in a warm room overnight.

Per portion Energy 242kcal/1005kJ; Protein 20.3g; Carbohydrate 3.1g, of which sugars 3.1g; Fat 16.5g, of which saturates 4.5g; Cholesterol 51mg; Calcium 17mg; Fibre 0.4g; Sodium 65mg.

Flower kidneys with ginger

Kidneys are revered for their nutritional properties and symbolism in China. Sliced artfully, they open up like flowers when cooked. Seasonings for kidneys tend to be robust to counteract their strong aroma and flavour. Use a strong Chinese cooking wine like Hsiao Hsing or Hua Teow.

1 Wash the kidney thoroughly and slice each in half lengthways to reveal the white membrane in each. Remove these completely, then soak the kidney halves in plenty of cold water for 10 minutes.

2 Cut each kidney half into 5cm/2in squares. Using a sharp knife, score the squares deeply in a criss-cross pattern. Put them on a plate and set them aside.

3 Heat the oil in a wok and fry the garlic and ginger for 40 seconds, until light brown. Add the spring onions and stir-fry for 30 seconds. Add the kidney slices and stir-fry rapidly over high heat for 1 minute, until they curl up to resemble flowers.

4 Add the oyster sauce, pepper and wine and bring rapidly to the boil. Add the cornflour mixture and stir over the heat until the sauce thickens. Spoon into a heated dish and serve.

Cook's tip If the kidneys have a very strong smell, soak them in milk instead of water, or simply soak them in water for twice as long as recommended in the recipe.

Serves 4

1 pig's kidney
30ml/2 tbsp vegetable oil
15ml/1 tbsp chopped garlic
15ml/1 tbsp chopped fresh
  root ginger
8 spring onions (scallions),
  cut in short lengths
30ml/2 tbsp oyster sauce
5–10ml/1–2 tsp ground black pepper
30ml/2 tbsp Chinese rice wine
10ml/2 tsp cornflour (cornstarch)
  mixed with 120ml/4fl oz/½ cup
  cold water

Per portion Energy 118kcal/491kJ; Protein 6.6g; Carbohydrate 6.4g, of which sugars 2.9g; Fat 6.6g, of which saturates 1g; Cholesterol 144mg; Calcium 15mg; Fibre 0.7g; Sodium 196mg.

Rice and noodles

As the world's most populous country, China would not have been able to sustain its one and a half billion people were it not for rice. Grown throughout most of the country, apart from the far north, it is the single most important element in almost every meal. No southerner would dream of sitting down to a meal without a bowl of fragrant, fluffy rice, providing the perfect foil for savoury dishes. Noodles made from rice or wheat are also popular. Infinitely versatile, they are used in many dishes, from simple stir-fries to luxurious treats.

Sweetly simple and stickily savoury

The Guangdong Delta and Hainan Island are among China's principal rice-growing areas. Rather than being a bland staple, the grain is regarded as a blank canvas on which many culinary portraits can be painted. In Shantou, rice soup is a favourite supper dish and cold, cooked rice is the basis of many ingenious fried creations. Clay Pot Rice is one such dish, redolent of the smoky flavour of dried oysters, and Seafood Fried Rice is briny and aromatic with fragrances of the sea.

Rice is also transformed into noodles in the south, although ones made from wheat from the north are also used. Tossed in oyster sauce or spicy chilli paste, they are consumed with relish. There can be marked differences in the tastes of noodle dishes, as more robust wheat noodles lend themselves to frying and boiling, while rice noodles, with a more silken nature, are treated with care, usually in soupy dishes and the occasional stir-fry.

Whatever dish is on order, accompanying ingredients provide the essential contrasts. Soft rice noodles with crunchy greens, sturdy wheat noodles with meat and poultry – these underscore the importance of balance within noodle cookery.

Serves 4

4 dried Chinese black mushrooms
150ml/¼ pint/⅔ cup boiling water
30ml/2 tbsp vegetable oil
2 garlic cloves, chopped
150g/5oz lean pork, finely sliced
150g/5oz pak choi (bok choy),
 finely sliced
30ml/2 tbsp peas, thawed
 if frozen
30ml/2 tbsp light soy sauce
5ml/1 tsp ground black pepper
5ml/1 tsp cornflour (cornstarch)
 mixed to a paste with 15ml/1 tbsp
 cold water
800g/1¾lb/7 cups cooked rice

Rice with mixed vegetables

A Cantonese staple, this originally called for ten different greens to be cooked with the rice. The tradition doesn't have to be followed to the letter for it to taste scrumptious, but it is a good idea to use several vegetables, plus a little meat for extra flavour.

1 Put the mushrooms in a heatproof bowl and pour over the boiling water. Leave to soak for 20–30 minutes, until soft. Using a slotted spoon, transfer the mushrooms to a board. Cut off and discard the stems. Chop the caps finely. Strain the soaking liquid into a measuring jug (cup) and set aside.

2 Heat the oil in a wok, add the garlic and fry over medium heat for 40 seconds, until light brown. Do not let it burn or it will become bitter. Add the pork and fry for 2 minutes.

3 Add the pak choi, peas and mushrooms. Stir to mix, then add the soy sauce, black pepper and the mushroom soaking liquid. Cook, stirring frequently, for 4 minutes.

4 Add the cornflour paste and stir until the mixture thickens slightly. Finally stir in the cooked rice. As soon as it is piping hot, spoon the mixture into a heated bowl and serve.

Per portion Energy 199kcal/834kJ; Protein 4.6g; Carbohydrate 43.4g, of which sugars 6.6g; Fat 0.7g, of which saturates 0.1g; Cholesterol 0mg; Calcium 23mg; Fibre 1.6g; Sodium 232mg.

Rice soup from Shantou

Although this dish contains many of the same ingredients as the rice congee cooked by the peoples of both Shantou and Guangzhou, it is actually very different: the rice stays relatively firm and every mouthful offers the contrasting textures of smooth soup and crunchy grain.

1 Using a sharp cook's knife, skin the fish, then cut it into small, thin pieces, removing any stray bones in the process. Pour the fish stock into a pan and bring it to the boil.

2 Put the rice in a colander and rinse it under cold running water. Drain well, then add to the fish stock. Simmer for 8–10 minutes or until the rice is just cooked; it should retain plenty of texture.

3 Add the pieces of fish, with the ground black pepper, and simmer for 2 minutes. Stir in the finely chopped Chinese celery, spoon into heated soup bowls and garnish with the fried shallots or garlic. Serve immediately.

Variation Crisp bread croutons can be used as a garnish instead of fried shallots or garlic.

Serves 4

200g/7oz white fish fillets
1.2 litres/2 pints/5 cups fresh
  fish stock
350g/12oz/1⅔ cups jasmine rice
  or long grain rice
5ml/1 tsp ground black pepper
leaves from 1 stalk Chinese celery,
  finely chopped
30ml/2 tbsp fried shallots or garlic,
  to garnish

Cook's tip Take care not to let the rice become mushy. It will continue to cook after the fish is added, so the initial boiling needs to be brief.

Per portion Energy 354kcal/1483kJ; Protein 16.1g; Carbohydrate 69.8g, of which sugars 0g; Fat 1g, of which saturates 0.2g; Cholesterol 23mg; Calcium 22mg; Fibre 0g; Sodium 394mg.

Clay pot rice with dried oysters

Dried oysters are a prime ingredient in Cantonese cooking. They are prized for their rich, smoky flavour, which is quite different to that of the fresh mollusc. When they are used in a recipe, there is no need for additional seasoning. They are also surprisingly meaty and add bulk to the dish. Here, they are combined with rice and tender chunks of Chinese sausage, and cooked in a pan before being served in a clay pot.

1 Put the rice in a large pan and pour over the water. Bring to the boil, then lower the heat and simmer for 8 minutes.

2 Meanwhile, heat the oil in a wok and fry the chopped onions for 2 minutes. Add the sliced root ginger, Chinese sausages, salt fish, dried oysters, sesame oil and pepper. Stir over the heat for 2 minutes, then stir in the soy sauce and oyster sauce.

3 When the rice is almost dry, but still bubbly on the top, stir in the onion mixture. Cover with a lid and cook for 8 minutes more.

4 Spoon the mixture into a preheated clay pot, if you have one (*see* Cook's tip), or on to a warmed serving platter if you don't. Serve immediately.

Cook's tip The clay pot isn't essential, but it does add a rustic touch. Clay pots are ideal for serving, but are not meant to be used for long cooking over a direct flame as they crack easily. Before spooning in the rice mixture, warm the pot briefly over a direct flame or in a preheated oven.

Serves 4

350g/12oz/1⅔ cups jasmine rice
600ml/1 pint/2½ cups water
30ml/2 tbsp vegetable oil
30ml/2 tbsp chopped onions
4 slices fresh root ginger
2 Chinese sausages,
  thinly sliced
100g/3¾ oz salt fish,
  fried and flaked
10 dried oysters
30ml/2 tbsp sesame oil
5ml/1 tsp black pepper
30ml/2 tbsp dark soy sauce
15ml/1 tbsp oyster sauce

Per portion Energy 472kcal/1971kJ; Protein 18.1g; Carbohydrate 71.7g, of which sugars 1g; Fat 12g, of which saturates 1.5g; Cholesterol 14mg; Calcium 90mg; Fibre 0.1g; Sodium 2544mg.

Seafood fried rice

This is one of those dishes that is found throughout China, although the ingredients will vary depending on the location. This simple version allows the flavour of the seafood to take centre stage. For festive occasions, luxury ingredients like lobster and scallops are often added.

1 Heat the oil in a wok and fry the garlic until golden brown. Do not let it burn or it will become bitter. Push the garlic aside to leave a clear space in the centre of the wok. Add the eggs and cook until they set to form an omelette.

2 Cut the omelette up roughly in the wok, and push it aside. Add the prawns and rice and stir rapidly for 5 minutes or until the shrimps are cooked and the rice is piping hot.

3 Sprinkle over the soy sauce. Add the black pepper and chopped spring onions. Toss to mix, then spoon into a bowl and serve garnished with the spring onion curls.

Cook's tip Spring onion (scallion) curls make a dramatic garnish. Trim 4 spring onions, removing the roots and bulbs. Using a sharp knife, finely shred the spring onions to within 2.5cm/1in of the root end. Place the shredded spring onions in a bowl of iced water and chill for at least 30 minutes or until the shredded ends have curled. Drain on kitchen paper.

Serves 4

30ml/2 tbsp vegetable oil
2 garlic cloves, crushed
2 eggs, lightly beaten
100g/3¾oz raw or cooked prawns
  (shrimps), peeled
800g/1¾lb/7 cups cold cooked rice
30ml/2 tbsp light soy sauce
2.5ml/½ tsp ground black pepper
2 spring onions (scallions),
  chopped
spring onion curls (*see* Cook's tip)
  to serve

Per portion Energy 386kcal/1629kJ; Protein 13.1g; Carbohydrate 62.6g, of which sugars 0.7g; Fat 11.1g, of which saturates 2.1g; Cholesterol 144mg; Calcium 73mg; Fibre 0.3g; Sodium 619mg.

Serves 4

2 spring onions (scallions), chopped

30ml/2 tbsp vegetable oil

3 eggs, lightly beaten

800g/1¾lb/7 cups cold cooked rice

150g/5oz roast pork or cooked ham,
 in 1cm/½in cubes

100g/3¾oz raw tiger prawns
 (jumbo shrimp), peeled

30ml/2 tbsp frozen green peas

30ml/2 tbsp light soy sauce

5ml/1 tsp ground black pepper

1 chicken stock cube

Per portion Energy 473kcal/1997kJ; Protein 25.3g; Carbohydrate 65.3g, of which sugars 2.5g; Fat 14.3g, of which saturates 2.9g; Cholesterol 238mg; Calcium 114mg; Fibre 1.3g; Sodium 1317mg.

Classic Cantonese fried rice

One of the most widely travelled Chinese dishes, this is a Cantonese invention, deriving from the pragmatic need to recycle leftovers. Some luxurious versions are packed with premium ingredients like crab meat and lobster. Others are really simple. What follows is a basic recipe, which can easily be adapted to suit the ingredients available.

1 Set aside about one-fifth of the spring onions for the garnish. Heat the oil in a wok and fry the remaining spring onions for 30 seconds. Push them aside to leave a clear space in the centre of the wok. Add the eggs and cook until they set to form an omelette.

2 Cut the omelette up roughly in the wok, then add the rice, pork or ham, and shrimps. Stir vigorously for 3 minutes, then add the peas. Stir in the soy sauce and black pepper, and crumble the stock cube over the surface.

3 Toss over the heat for 3 minutes more, or until the rice is piping hot all the way through. Spoon into a bowl and garnish with the reserved spring onions. Serve immediately.

Glutinous rice in a lotus leaf

Serving food in a leaf reveals the enduring connection the southern Chinese have with the land. For maximum impact, serve this piping hot and open it at the table with a dramatic flourish. The aromatic steam released at the critical moment will delight guests and whet their appetites for the delicious rice mixture hidden within the rice parcel.

1 Rinse the glutinous rice under running water until the water runs clear, then soak it in a bowl of water for 2 hours. Meanwhile, soak the mushrooms in a separate bowl of boiling water for 30 minutes.

2 Drain the rice, tip it into a bowl and stir in the salt. Line a large steamer with clean muslin (cheesecloth) and spoon in the rice. Cover and steam over a wok of boiling water for 15 minutes. Remove and set aside.

3 Soak the lotus leaf in warm water for 15 minutes. Drain the mushrooms, cut off and discard the stems, then chop the caps finely.

4 Heat the oil in a wok and fry the garlic for 40 seconds. Add the chicken and Chinese sausage. Stir-fry for 2 minutes, then add the mushrooms, chestnuts, light and dark soy sauce, oyster sauce, sesame oil, spring onions and black pepper. Stir-fry for 2 minutes.

5 Sprinkle over 15ml/1 tbsp water, add the rice and cook for 2–3 minutes more. Drain the lotus leaf. Lay it on a flat surface and pile the fried ingredients in the centre. Gather up the sides of the leaf and fold into a large bundle. Tuck the sides in firmly.

6 Prepare a steamer. Place the filled lotus leaf, seam side down, on a plate that will fit inside the steamer. Steam for 10 minutes. Serve with chilli sauce.

Serves 4

400g/14oz/2 cups glutinous rice
4 dried Chinese black mushrooms
15ml/1 tbsp salt
1 large lotus leaf, about 50cm/20in in diameter
30ml/2 tbsp vegetable oil
2 garlic cloves, crushed
200g/7oz skinless, boneless chicken, diced
1 Chinese sausage, finely sliced
8 drained canned Chinese chestnuts
30ml/2 tbsp light soy sauce
15ml/1 tbsp dark soy sauce
30ml/2 tbsp oyster sauce
30ml/2 tbsp sesame oil
30ml/2 tbsp chopped spring onions (scallions)
5ml/1 tsp ground black pepper
chilli sauce, to serve

Per portion Energy 596kcal/2488kJ; Protein 23.6g; Carbohydrate 79.5g, of which sugars 2.7g; Fat 19.3g, of which saturates 3.9g; Cholesterol 44mg; Calcium 45mg; Fibre 0.9g; Sodium 979mg.

Buddhist vegetarian noodles

During Buddhist festivals, this dish takes centre stage as temple chefs cook huge cauldrons of it to serve to devotees, free of charge. It is a simple dish, redolent with flavour and with a lovely crunchy texture.

1 Soak the dried mushrooms in a bowl of boiling water for 20–30 minutes until soft. Meanwhile soak the beancurd wafers and rice vermicelli until soft, following the directions on the packets.

2 Drain the mushrooms thoroughly, then cut off and discard the stems and slice the caps into thin strips. Drain the beancurd wafers and slice them thinly. Drain the noodles and set them aside.

3 Heat the oil in a wok and fry the garlic for 40 seconds, until light brown. Add the onion and stir-fry for 2 minutes, then add the beansprouts, bamboo shoots, beans and mushrooms. Stir-fry for 1 minute, then stir in the hoisin sauce, oyster sauce, soy sauce and sesame oil.

4 Add the beancurd wafers to the wok and stir-fry for 2 minutes more. Add the noodles and pour in the water. Toss over the heat for about 4 minutes, until all the ingredients are cooked and the mixture is well blended. Spoon into a bowl and serve.

Cook's tips
• The mushroom soaking water can be substituted for some of the water added at the end of cooking. Strain it first, to remove any pieces of grit.
• Sweet beancurd wafers are crisp, brown slices, sold in small packets. Each measures about 12.5 x 5cm (5 x 2in). They are called *tim choke* in Cantonese. If you deep-fry them without soaking them first, they can be crumbled on to the cooked dish as a garnish.

Serves 4

10 dried Chinese black mushrooms
4 pieces sweet dried
  beancurd wafers
300g/11oz rice vermicelli
45ml/3 tbsp vegetable oil
30ml/2 tbsp crushed garlic
1 large onion, thinly sliced
100g/3¾oz/½ cup beansprouts
115g/4oz drained canned bamboo
  shoots, sliced into thin strips
115g/4oz Chinese long beans
  or green beans, sliced into
  thin strips
30ml/2 tbsp hoi sin sauce
30ml/2 tbsp oyster sauce
30ml/2 tbsp dark soy sauce
45ml/3 tbsp sesame oil
400ml/14fl oz/1⅔ cups water

Per portion Energy 509kcal/2116kJ; Protein 12.7g; Carbohydrate 73g, of which sugars 9.9g; Fat 18.6g, of which saturates 2.2g; Cholesterol 0mg; Calcium 200mg; Fibre 3.3g; Sodium 726mg.

Silver threads of longevity

The 'silver threads' of the recipe title are cellophane noodles. In China these symbolize longevity and are often served at birthdays and other special occasions. Also known as glass noodles, transparent vermicelli or translucent noodles, they are made from green mung beans and are widely used in both hot and cold dishes. Here they are teamed with lily buds, which contribute a mild, sweet taste and crunchy texture.

1 Soak the lily buds in a bowl of warm water for 30 minutes or until soft. Meanwhile, soak the cellophane noodles in a separate bowl of warm water for 15 minutes.

2 Drain the lily buds, rinse them under cold water and drain again. Snip off the hard ends. Drain the noodles. Using a pair of scissors or a sharp knife, chop the strands into shorter lengths for easier handling.

3 Heat the oil in a wok and fry the garlic for 40 seconds. Do not let the garlic burn. Add the beansprouts. Stir-fry vigorously for 1 minute. Add the lily buds and the noodles and toss over the heat for 2 minutes.

4 Add the oyster sauce, soy sauce and sesame oil. Pour in the water. Continue to toss over the heat until the liquid is hot and the noodles and lily buds are coated in the mixture. Spoon into a heated serving dish and garnish with the chopped coriander. Serve immediately.

Serves 4

50g/2oz dried lily buds
150g/5oz cellophane noodles
45ml/3 tbsp vegetable oil
30ml/2 tbsp crushed garlic
100g/3¾oz/½ cup beansprouts
30ml/2 tbsp oyster sauce
30ml/2 tbsp light soy sauce
45ml/3 tbsp sesame oil
200ml/7fl oz/scant 1 cup water
chopped fresh coriander (cilantro),
  to garnish

Per portion Energy 307kcal/1274kJ; Protein 3.3g; Carbohydrate 34.8g, of which sugars 3.4g; Fat 16.7g, of which saturates 2.2g; Cholesterol 0mg; Calcium 15mg; Fibre 0.6g; Sodium 663mg.

Serves 4

400g/14oz dry wheat flour noodles
200g/7oz choi sum
250g/9oz roast pork, thinly sliced
60ml/4 tbsp chilli and garlic sauce
30ml/2 tbsp vegetable or sesame oil
30ml/2 tbsp light soy sauce
30ml/2 tbsp tomato sauce (ketchup)
Prawn Wonton Soup, to serve
  (optional)

Variation Spinach, cos or romaine lettuce can be used instead of choi sum, or use beansprouts.

Per portion Energy 208kcal/879kJ; Protein 18.9g; Carbohydrate 26.6g, of which sugars 7.1g; Fat 3.5g, of which saturates 0.9g; Cholesterol 39mg; Calcium 101mg; Fibre 2.3g; Sodium 975mg.

Chilli noodles

Street stalls and tea houses all over Hong Kong almost always have this on their menus, each establishment having a slightly different version from the next, depending on the class of diner. Humble places offer basic noodles tossed in chilli sauce with slices of roast pork. More upmarket eateries add lavish accents like oyster sauce and sesame oil and even offer wonton soup on the side. This recipe is one of the more luxurious versions.

1 Cook the noodles in boiling water until tender, following the package directions for timing. Drain the noodles and put them in a bowl.

2 Cut the choi sum into bitesize pieces. Bring a pan of water to the boil, add the greens and blanch for 1 minute. Drain and mix with the noodles.

3 Halve the roast pork slices if necessary; the aim is to have about 32 pieces of pork in all. Set aside.

4 In a bowl, mix the chilli and garlic sauce with the oil, soy sauce and tomato sauce. Add to the noodles and greens and toss lightly to coat. Top with the pork. Serve at once, with the Prawn Wonton Soup on the side, if you like.

Lobster noodles

Hong Kong chefs constantly invent and innovate, striving to create dishes at the cutting edge to impress gourmet taste buds. This one is in the luxury league. Restaurants present this dish with great fanfare, with the lobster sitting in all its pink-shelled glory on top of the cooked noodles.

1 If the lobster is live, place it in a plastic bag and put it in the freezer for 5–7 hours. Bring a large pan of water to the boil, add the comatose lobster and cook for 10 minutes or until the shell has turned scarlet. Remove and set aside to cool. Heat a separate pan of water and cook the noodles according to the instructions on the packet. Drain and set aside.

2 When the lobster is cool enough to handle, use a sharp knife to cut off the head and the tip of the tail. Rinse and set aside for the garnish. Twist off the claws and set aside.

3 Using a sharp pair of poultry shears or strong scissors, cut down the shell from the top to the tail. Remove the lobster meat, and slice it into rounds. Remove the meat from the claws and legs. Set all the lobster meat aside.

4 Heat the oil in a wok and fry the garlic for 40 seconds. Add the beansprouts and toss over the heat for 2 minutes. Add the noodles, water, oyster sauce, black pepper and sesame oil and cook, stirring, for 2 minutes.

5 Add the lobster slices and toss lightly. Arrange on a large oval plate, making sure that the lobster pieces are fairly prominent. Decorate with the lobster head and tail.

Serves 4

1 large live or freshly cooked
  lobster, about 1kg/2¼lb
400g/14oz dried egg
  noodles
30ml/2 tbsp vegetable oil
15ml/1 tbsp crushed garlic
100g/3¾oz/½ cup beansprouts
200ml/7fl oz/scant 1 cup
  water
30ml/2 tbsp oyster sauce
5ml/1 tsp ground black
  pepper
30ml/2 tbsp sesame oil

Per portion Energy 501kcal/2110kJ; Protein 29.9g; Carbohydrate 56.9g, of which sugars 4g; Fat 18.8g, of which saturates 3.5g; Cholesterol 123mg; Calcium 83mg; Fibre 2.6g; Sodium 559mg.

Oyster sauce noodles with chicken

Noodles are usually cooked with other ingredients, and eaten not as accompaniments, but as snacks or light meals. This recipe is a basic one for rice noodles and can be adapted to include other types of meat, seafood or vegetables, depending on your preference.

1 Slice the chicken breast into thin strips. If using fresh *hor fun*, separate the noodles. If they stick together, steam them lightly first. If using dried rice noodle sticks, soak them in boiling water until soft, then drain well.

2 Heat the oil in a wok and fry the crushed garlic over medium heat until golden brown. Do not let it burn.

3 Add the chicken strips and stir-fry over high heat for 3 minutes. Add the noodles, spring onions, water, oyster sauce, pepper and sesame oil. Toss over high heat for 2 minutes.

4 Tip into a heated bowl or individual bowls, garnish with more chopped spring onions and serve immediately.

Variation Rice noodles, preferably the fresh ribbon ones called *hor fun*, are preferred in Cantonese cooking but there is no reason why egg or plain wheat noodles should not be used for this recipe.

Serves 4

250g/9oz skinless chicken
 breast fillets
400g/14oz fresh hor fun (flat rice
 noodles) or dried rice noodle sticks
30ml/2 tbsp vegetable oil
15ml/1 tbsp crushed garlic
2 spring onions (scallions), cut
 in 2.5cm/1in strips, plus extra
 for garnishing
200ml/7fl oz/scant 1 cup water
30ml/2 tbsp oyster sauce
5ml/1 tsp ground black pepper
30ml/2 tbsp sesame oil

Per portion Energy 536kcal/2237kJ; Protein 20.4g; Carbohydrate 83.5g, of which sugars 1.9g; Fat 11.9g, of which saturates 1.7g; Cholesterol 44mg; Calcium 24mg; Fibre 0.4g; Sodium 133mg.

Vegetables

The fertile fields of southern China produce a wonderful array of fresh indigenous ingredients, including a wide range of vegetables. Although rarely served on their own, as they are in the West, vegetables are included in most savoury dishes. The ones in this chapter include a number of quick stir-fries featuring a particular vegetable. Mixed with aromatics and often some fish or meat, they encapsulate the desired balance of taste and texture that southern Chinese cooks strive to attain.

Flash-fried and fresh-flavoured

Chinese people are not given to eating vegetables raw, and most are usually fried. Stir-fried lettuce is given a briny fillip with conpoy (scallop) sauce. More robust greens, such as kai lan, are also enjoyed and, served Hong-Kong style with oyster sauce, make a star appearance at restaurants both in Hong Kong and around the world.

Beansprouts grow like weeds and show up in numerous dishes. Stir-fried and flavoured with salt fish and sesame oil, they are highly revered. Bitter melon or gourd, while a marrow of acquired taste, features in the Guangzhou dish of Stir-Fried Bitter Gourd. Root vegetables like yam (*taro*) are played with at will, and Hakka cooks are adept at bringing out its texture and flavour with inventive dishes like Abacus Beads, in which the vegetable is cooked, mashed and shaped into beads that represent the abacus.

Water convolvulus, while indigenous to South-east Asia, has been incorporated into the southern Chinese repertoire. Grown in swampy areas, it has hollow stalks and delicate leaves that demand quick cooking. It goes by several names, including water spinach, swamp cabbage and morning glory.

Serves 4–6

1 head Chinese leaves
  (Chinese cabbage)
30ml/2 tbsp sesame oil
300ml/½ pint/1¼ cups water
5ml/1 tsp ground black pepper
30ml/2 tbsp light soy sauce

Braised Chinese leaves

Chinese leaves, also known as Chinese cabbage, taste delicious in a salad or stir-fry and need little seasoning apart from soy sauce as they have a natural sweet flavour. This dish is somewhat soupy, since the leaves contribute extra liquid. It is often served with rice porridge or congee, and keeps well.

1 Slice the Chinese leaves lengthways and remove the hard tip and core. Cut in 2.5cm/1in slices and place in a colander. Rinse under cold water, then drain thoroughly.

2 Mix the oil, water, black pepper and soy sauce in a wok. Bring to simmering point, add the Chinese leaves and braise for 15 minutes over medium heat. Spoon into a heated dish and serve immediately.

Cook's tip Don't confuse Chinese leaves with bok choy, which has thick white stems topped by glossy green leaves.

Per portion Energy 58kcal/239kJ; Protein 1.3g; Carbohydrate 4.6g, of which sugars 4.5g; Fat 3.8g, of which saturates 0.5g; Cholesterol 0mg; Calcium 42mg; Fibre 1.8g; Sodium 362mg.

Mustard greens with oyster sauce

Also known as mustard cabbage (gai choy in Cantonese) mustard greens have thick, curved, ribbed stalks and ruffled bright green leaves. Shantou people are inordinately fond of this vegetable and usually serve it with congee for breakfast or lunch. In China, the bulk of the crop is salted and preserved.

1 Cut off any fibrous bits from the stalks of the mustard greens, then cut both the stalks and the leaves into bite-size pieces. Rinse thoroughly in cold water, then drain.

2 Bring a pan of water to the boil. Add the greens and blanch for 2 minutes, then drain and pat dry with kitchen paper or a clean dish towel.

3 Heat the oil in a wok. Add the garlic and fry until golden brown. Do not let the garlic burn or it will become bitter.

4 Add the blanched greens to the wok. Sprinkle over the oyster sauce, then add the water. Cook over high heat for 2–3 minutes, tossing constantly with two spoons or spatulas, so that they cook evenly. Spoon into a heated dish and serve immediately with rice.

Cook's tip Mustard greens are widely grown and are especially popular with home gardeners and allotment holders. Look for them at farmers' markets or Chinese food stores.

Serves 4

500g/1¼lb mustard greens
30ml/2 tbsp vegetable oil
30ml/2 tbsp crushed garlic
30ml/2 tbsp oyster sauce
200ml/7fl oz/scant 1 cup water
cooked rice or congee, to serve

Per portion Energy 89kcal/369kJ; Protein 3.6g; Carbohydrate 4.2g, of which sugars 4g; Fat 6.5g, of which saturates 0.8g; Cholesterol 0mg; Calcium 214mg; Fibre 2.7g; Sodium 297mg.

Stir-fried kai lan

There was a time when this popular Chinese vegetable was practically unobtainable outside its country of origin, but airfreight has changed all that and most Chinese food stores now stock it. Known as Chinese broccoli – kai lan in Cantonese – it actually bears no resemblance to broccoli, being more closely related to kale. It has dark green leaves and crunchy stems.

1 Separate the kai lan leaves from the stalks. Cut each leaf in half. Trim the stalks, then peel them thinly, removing any tough portions of outer skin. Slice each stalk diagonally in half.

2 Bring a pan of water to the boil and blanch the kai lan leaves for 1 minute. Drain immediately in a colander, and refresh under cold water. This will help to retain the vegetable's bright green colour. Drain well. Repeat the process with the kai lan stalks, keeping leaves and stalks separate.

3 Heat the oil in a wok and fry the ginger and garlic until the latter is golden brown. Add the kai lan stalks and stir-fry for 1 minute. Add the leaves, stir well, then add the oyster sauce and wine. Stir rapidly over the heat for 2 minutes, spoon into a dish and serve immediately.

Variation Tenderstem broccoli, now available in most supermarkets, comes close to kai lan in flavour and texture. Purple sprouting broccoli or chard can be used as a substitute.

Serves 4

350g/12oz kai lan (Chinese broccoli)
30ml/2 tbsp vegetable oil
30ml/2 tbsp shredded fresh
  root ginger
30ml/2 tbsp crushed garlic
30ml/2 tbsp oyster sauce
30ml/2 tbsp Chinese wine

Per portion Energy 108kcal/448kJ; Protein 5g; Carbohydrate 5.9g, of which sugars 3.7g; Fat 6.4g, of which saturates 0.8g; Cholesterol 0mg; Calcium 53mg; Fibre 2.9g; Sodium 131mg.

Serves 4

4 pieces conpoy (*see* Cook's tip)
200ml/7fl oz/scant 1 cup warm water
2 heads cos or romaine lettuce
15ml/1 tbsp vegetable oil
15ml/1 tbsp chopped fresh root ginger
2 garlic cloves, chopped
30ml/2 tbsp Chinese wine

Per portion Energy 131kcal/549kJ; Protein 12.4g;
Carbohydrate 3.5g, of which sugars 1.8g; Fat 6.7g,
of which saturates 1g; Cholesterol 24mg; Calcium
43mg; Fibre 0.9g; Sodium 94mg.

Hot lettuce with conpoy sauce

Chinese cooks rarely eat vegetables raw, even when using the most tender salad-type greens. Stir-frying them with aromatics like garlic and ginger is popular, and a liquid is often added toward the end of cooking to soften the ingredients slightly and provide a tasty sauce.

1 Put the pieces of conpoy in a bowl and pour over the warm water. Soak for 2–3 hours until soft. Meanwhile, shred the lettuce, put in a colander and rinse it under cold water. Drain well, then dry the lettuce thoroughly in a clean dish towel.

2 Drain the conpoy, reserving the soaking liquid. Use a sharp knife to shred the pieces finely.

3 Heat the oil in a wok and fry the ginger and garlic for 40 seconds, until light brown. Add the lettuce and stir-fry over high heat for 1 minute.

4 Add the conpoy, with the reserved soaking liquid. Bring to a quick simmer, stirring constantly, for 2 minutes. Tip into a serving dish and serve immediately.

Cook's tip Conpoy is an expensive shellfish closely related to the sea scallop. It is only available dried and is used as a master seasoning in a variety of dishes, including a version of the humble congee. If you do not have time to soak it as described in the recipe, soften it by heating it in the measured water in a microwave on High for 1 minute.

Stir-fried bitter gourd

Also known as bitter melon, this pale green vegetable has a distinctive, warty skin. It has a sweet and fragrant smell, but a rather bitter flavour. Salting the raw vegetable helps to remove some of the bitterness and promotes a crunchy texture. Cooking it with hoisin and oyster sauces and a little sugar also helps to offset any astringency.

1 Slice off about 1cm/½in from either end of the bitter gourd. Cut it in half lengthways and scoop out the white pith and soft pink seeds.

2 Cut the gourd diagonally into 1cm/½in slices. Spread these out in a colander, sprinkle with the salt and let it stand in a sink for 30 minutes.

3 Rinse under cold water to remove the excess salt, then drain. Take handfuls of the now slightly softened bitter gourd and squeeze out as much moisture as possible.

4 Heat the oil in a wok and fry the garlic until golden brown. Do not let it burn or it will taste bitter. Add the pieces of bitter gourd to the pan and stir-fry for 1 minute.

5 Stir in the hoisin and oyster sauces, then add the water and sugar. Bring to the boil over high heat, simmer for 2 minutes until the sauce has reduced slightly, then spoon into a bowl and serve.

Variation For a more substantial dish, add a handful of cooked peeled prawns (shrimp) or cooked crab meat just before serving. Their tender meat will contrast beautifully with the crisp, slightly bitter vegetable.

Serves 4

1 bitter gourd, about 300g/11oz
5ml/1 tsp salt
30ml/2 tbsp vegetable oil
15ml/1 tbsp crushed garlic
30ml/2 tbsp hoisin sauce
30ml/2 tbsp oyster sauce
200ml/7fl oz/scant 1 cup water
2.5ml/½ tsp sugar

Cook's tips

• Traditional Chinese Medicine (TCM) regards bitter gourd as a yin or cooling vegetable and values it for its curative properties.
• Be sure to buy the large Chinese gourds, which are around 30cm/12in long, and not the smaller ones that are sold in Indian and Caribbean stores.

Per portion Energy 80kcal/331kJ; Protein 1.6g; Carbohydrate 5.6g, of which sugars 5.4g; Fat 5.8g, of which saturates 0.7g; Cholesterol 0mg; Calcium 21mg; Fibre 0.8g; Sodium 696mg.

Serves 4

400g/14oz water convolvulus
 (swamp cabbage)
30ml/2 tbsp vegetable oil
30ml/2 tbsp chopped garlic
200g/7oz raw prawns
 (shrimp), peeled
30ml/2 tbsp whole preserved
 yellow beans
2 fresh red chillies, seeded
 and sliced
90ml/6 tbsp water

Stir-fried water convolvulus

Water convolvulus is an all-year-round tropical vegetable that appears in many South-east Asian cuisines. It is a favourite with the people of southern China, who usually stir-fry it with chopped garlic. Cantonese cooks also sometimes add preserved beancurd, while in Hakka cuisine yellow bean paste or whole preserved yellow beans is added, as here.

1 Slice the water convolvulus stalks thinly and pluck off the leaves. Wash in plenty of water as the vegetable is grown in brackish water and mud is sometimes trapped in crevices in the stalks. Drain well and leave to air-dry or pat dry with kitchen paper.

2 Heat the oil in a wok and fry the garlic for 40 seconds, until golden brown. Add the prawns, yellow beans and chillies and toss together over the heat for 1 minute.

3 Add the water. Cover the wok with a lid, or improvize and make one from foil. Cook for 3 minutes until the leaves and stalks of the water convolvulus shrink and turn dark green. Tip into a heated bowl and serve immediately.

Per portion Energy 138kcal/574kJ; Protein 12.1g; Carbohydrate 8.6g, of which sugars 5.2g; Fat 6.2g, of which saturates 0.7g; Cholesterol 98mg; Calcium 97mg; Fibre 2.7g; Sodium 104mg.

Beansprouts with salt fish

*This simple peasant dish has been elevated to gourmet status. The cardinal rule is to use the best salt fish available, ideally salted fillets of snapper or an expensive tropical fish called threadfin (*ma yeow yu *in Cantonese). If this is not obtainable, the closest substitute is salt cod.*

1 Cut the salt fish into small chunks. Heat the oil in a wok and fry the pieces of salt fish until fragrant and slightly brittle. With a slotted spoon, transfer them to a board. Let them cool slightly, then shred them roughly.

2 Wash the beansprouts, drain them thoroughly and remove any green husks. Cut the spring onions into 5cm/2in lengths.

3 Pour off all but 30ml/2 tbsp of the oil from the wok. Heat the remaining oil and fry the garlic until golden brown. Add the beansprouts and salt fish and stir rapidly for 2 minutes.

4 Add the spring onions and stir-fry for 1 minute. Drizzle over the soy sauce, stir for 1 minute more and serve immediately.

Serves 4

100g/3¾oz salt fish fillet
60ml/4 tbsp vegetable oil
600g/1lb 6oz/2⅓ cups beansprouts
2 spring onions (scallions)
30ml/2 tbsp crushed garlic
15ml/1 tbsp light soy sauce

Cook's tip Sprout your own soya beans, if possible. If you do buy the sprouts, however, look for ones with large heads, as these are the healthiest option.

Per portion Energy 185kcal/772kJ; Protein 13.2g; Carbohydrate 6.5g, of which sugars 3.7g; Fat 12.1g, of which saturates 1.5g; Cholesterol 0mg; Calcium 68mg; Fibre 2.3g; Sodium 2157mg.

Abacus beads

Most people are familiar with the abacus, the ancient Chinese counting instrument consisting of a wire-strung frame on which beads are threaded. Many Chinese storekeepers still prefer the abacus to the calculator and use one with great dexterity. In a cultural context, the abacus, and this dish, symbolizes prosperity. Hakka people traditionally serve it at Lunar New Year celebrations to bring good fortune for the year ahead. The abacus beads are represented by discs of boiled yam.

1 Make the yam beads. Peel the yam and cut it into small chunks. Place in a steamer and cook over simmering water for 30 minutes or until very soft. Cool, then place in a food processor. Add the water and salt. Process until very smooth.

2 Add the rice flour and cornflour or tapioca flour to the yam paste. Continue to process the mixture until all the ingredients combine to form a smooth dough. Transfer to a lightly floured board.

3 Pinch off pieces of dough, each the size of a walnut, and roll and shape into little discs. Press each disc in the middle on both sides to make small dimples. Place on a lightly oiled plate and steam for 10 minutes.

4 Meanwhile, heat the oil in a wok and fry the garlic for 40 seconds, until light brown. Add the prawns and stir-fry for 2 minutes. Add the celery, black pepper, soy sauce, sugar, sesame oil and water. Stir for 1 minute, then add the steamed yam beads. Stir until well mixed, spoon into a bowl and serve hot.

Serves 4–6

30ml/2 tbsp vegetable oil
4 garlic cloves, sliced
200g/7oz raw prawns
  (shrimp), peeled
1 Chinese celery stick,
  roughly chopped
5ml/1 tsp ground black pepper
30ml/2 tbsp light soy sauce
5ml/1 tsp sugar
30ml/2 tbsp sesame oil
90ml/6 tbsp water

For the yam beads
300g/11oz yam (taro)
75ml/5 tbsp water
2.5ml/½ tsp salt
50g/2oz/½ cup rice flour
15ml/1 tbsp cornflour (cornstarch)
  or tapioca flour

Per portion Energy 201kcal/844kJ; Protein 7.9g; Carbohydrate 25.7g, of which sugars 0.8g; Fat 7.8g, of which saturates 1.1g; Cholesterol 65mg; Calcium 41mg; Fibre 1.1g; Sodium 425mg.

Sweet things

The sweet foods in this chapter are not necessarily served at the end to a meal in south China, or indeed anywhere in the country. The communal Chinese meal has never been structured to embrace desserts as a final flourish. More often than not, only Chinese tea and perhaps some fresh fruit are served as a palate cleanser. Sweet things are generally regarded as between-meal snacks, or for special and festive occasions like the Lunar New Year, when sweet buns and dumplings of every hue and shape make a splendid show as offerings to deities.

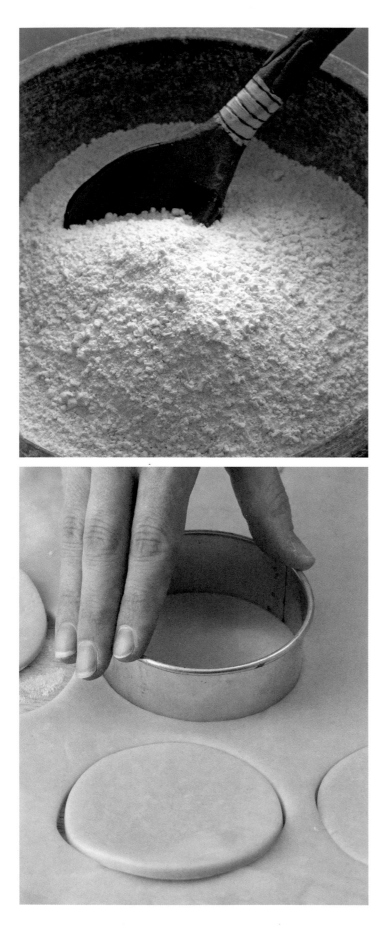

Silkily smooth and crisply crunchy

Although the range of sweet cakes, puddings and assorted bean-paste bakes and buns eaten in south China is wide, they have not had much impact outside the country, possibly because these items are so different from the wheat flour and butter-based products of the western genre. Instead, Chinese restaurants outside the country are more likely to showcase pan-Asian hybrids like banana fritters and toffee apples, both originating from South-east Asia.

Most Chinese desserts are made from rice flour or another type of flour, such as water chestnut flour. Even sweet buns based on wheat flour doughs invariably include a distinctively Chinese substance like sweet bean paste, almond paste or sesame paste.

Dairy products are rarely, if ever, used, either in the dough or the filling. Even the famous Egg Tarts from Macau, which use Cheddar cheese, are a Portuguese creation dating from when the island was a Portuguese enclave in the 16th century.

Other popular desserts include jellies made from a seaweed extract called agar agar, and fruits, nuts and seeds in a simple sugar syrup, as in Lotus Seeds in Syrup.

Serves 4

750ml/1¼ pints/3 cups water
100g/3¾oz rock sugar
40 drained canned lotus seeds
40 drained canned ginkgo nuts
6 pieces preserved sweet
winter melon

Lotus seeds in syrup

Within the pantheon of Chinese herbal remedies, lotus seeds are believed to aid blood circulation and stimulate sluggish appetites, while ginkgo nuts have for thousands of years been famed for their curative properties. Both turn up in herbal soups and sweet drinks like this one.

1 Put the water in a pan. Bring to the boil and add the rock sugar. Stir over the heat until it has dissolved.

2 Taste the syrup for sweetness and add more sugar if necessary. Stir in the lotus seeds and nuts with the preserved sweet winter melon. Simmer for 20 minutes. Serve hot or cold.

Per portion Energy 531kcal/2209kJ; Protein 5g; Carbohydrate 42.8g, of which sugars 42.4g; Fat 38.9g, of which saturates 5.6g; Cholesterol 0mg; Calcium 43mg; Fibre 3.4g; Sodium 143mg.

Almond jelly

This dish from Hong Kong is traditionally made using soaked, ground whole almonds. This simplified version, using almond extract, requires less effort and gives results that are just as good. The jelly has a subtle, sweet flavour that is popular with children and adults alike.

1 Pour the cold water into a pan and add the agar agar strips. Sprinkle the gelatine on the surface. Heat gently, stirring until all the agar agar and gelatine has dissolved.

2 Add the sugar. Simmer, stirring constantly, until the sugar has dissolved, then stir in the evaporated milk and almond extract.

3 Rinse a jelly mould with cold water and stand it upside down to drain. Stir the almond mixture well, then pour it into the jelly mould. Leave to cool, then chill until set.

4 Loosen the sides of the jelly with a knife, then unmould it on to a serving plate. If it is reluctant to leave the mould, dip it briefly in warm water before trying again. Serve with fruit cocktail or lychees.

Serves 6–8

750ml/1¼ pints/3 cups cold water
25g/1oz agar agar strips
15ml/1 tbsp powdered gelatine
300g/10oz/1½ cups sugar
150ml/¼ pint/⅔ cup evaporated milk
15ml/1 tbsp almond extract
fruit cocktail or lychees, to serve

Per portion Energy 181kcal/768kJ; Protein 4.8g; Carbohydrate 41.1g, of which sugars 41.1g; Fat 0.8g, of which saturates 0.5g; Cholesterol 3mg; Calcium 69mg; Fibre 0g; Sodium 24mg.

Egg tarts

These simple yet delectable little tarts clearly demonstrate the hybrid Portuguese-Chinese nature of the food from Macau, which was a Portuguese enclave for over four hundred years. Over the centuries, this sweet snack has become a favourite throughout the region and abroad and is probably the only Chinese dessert that contains cheese. The ingredients used outside China can vary, however, with the cheese often being omitted and a dash of ground cinnamon being sprinkled over the top.

1 Pour the cream into a large, heavy pan and stir in the sugar. Heat gently, stirring continuously, until the sugar dissolves, then bring to the boil. Be careful not to let the mixture stick on the bottom or it will burn.

2 Add the cheese to the cream mixture and cook over low heat until the cheese melts and the mixture is smooth. Remove the pan from the heat and set aside until the mixture has cooled a little.

3 In a bowl, beat the eggs lightly with the salt. Add to the cream mixture with the vanilla extract and milk. Strain through a fine sieve (strainer) into a clean bowl.

4 Preheat the oven to 200°C/400°F/Gas 6. On a lightly floured surface, roll out the pastry to a thickness of around 3mm/⅛in, and cut out 24 rounds with a pastry cutter. Fit these into two 12-hole tartlet tins (muffin pans), pressing them down gently.

5 Pour the filling into the pastry cases, filling them almost to the top. Bake for 20 minutes or until the filling has set and is golden brown. Remove from the pans and cool on wire racks. Serve warm.

Makes 24

150ml/¼ pint/⅔ cup single (light) cream or whipping cream
75ml/5 tbsp sugar
45g/1½oz mild Cheddar cheese, grated
3 large eggs, lightly beaten
pinch of salt
2.5ml/½ tsp vanilla extract
175ml/6fl oz/¾ cup milk
450g/1lb shortcrust pastry, thawed if frozen

Cook's tips
• Beat the eggs lightly. If they are over-beaten the filling will rise too much.
• If not eaten immediately, the tarts can be kept in an airtight tin for a day or two. Reheat them in an oven preheated to 180°C/350°F/Gas 4 for 10 minutes.

Per portion Energy 131kcal/549kJ; Protein 3g; Carbohydrate 12.5g, of which sugars 3.9g; Fat 8g, of which saturates 3.1g; Cholesterol 37mg; Calcium 50mg; Fibre 0.4g; Sodium 104mg.

Water chestnut cake

That this has become a quintessential Cantonese dessert says a lot for the free exchange of culinary ideas in China, since it originated in the north. Water chestnuts give the cake a delightful crunchy texture. It is sometimes fried after being steamed, but is just as delicious cold. The unusual sweet-savoury flavour makes it equally suitable for serving as a dessert or a snack.

1 Put the water chestnut flour in a bowl and stir in the milk with a wooden spoon to make a smooth paste. Set aside.

2 In a food processor, grind the water chestnuts to a fine pulp. Add the oil, sugar and water and process until well mixed. Scrape into a pan and bring to the boil.

3 Add half the water chestnut flour paste to the pan. Simmer, stirring, for 5 minutes. Remove from the heat and leave to cool for 10 minutes. Add the remaining paste, a little at a time, stirring constantly. Return to the heat and cook, stirring, for 3 minutes, until it has the consistency of thick cream.

4 Spoon the mixture into a tray or pan which will fit in a steamer, then smooth the top with a moistened knife. Steam for 30 minutes. Remove and leave to cool and set; it will be quite firm. Cut into squares and serve cold or fry lightly in oil to serve warm.

Serves 6

150g/5oz/1¼ cups water
  chestnut flour
200ml/7fl oz/scant 1 cup milk
200g/7oz can water
  chestnuts, drained
60ml/4 tbsp corn or vegetable oil
150g/5oz/¾ cup caster
  (superfine) sugar
400ml/14fl oz/1⅔ cups water

Per portion Energy 190kcal/800kJ; Protein 2.2g; Carbohydrate 29g, of which sugars 28.4g; Fat 8.1g, of which saturates 1.3g; Cholesterol 2mg; Calcium 60mg; Fibre 0.5g; Sodium 18mg.

Makes about 12

200g/7oz/1¾ cups bun flour or
    self-raising (self-rising) flour
5ml/1 tsp sugar
pinch of salt
15g/½oz easy-blend (rapid-rise)
    dried yeast
120ml/4fl oz/½ cup warm water
1 can sweet bean paste (about
    300g/11oz depending on the brand)

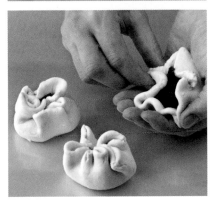

Per portion Energy 112kcal/477kJ; Protein 4.5g;
Carbohydrate 24.1g, of which sugars 5g; Fat 0.4g,
of which saturates 0.1g; Cholesterol 0mg; Calcium
36mg; Fibre 1.5g; Sodium 3mg.

Bean paste buns

There are scores of different dumplings in the dim sum repertoire, with many of them using the same pastry base and varying only in the fillings they contain. These buns use the same dough as Roast Pork Dumplings, but instead of pork, the filling is a sweet bean paste called tau sa, *which is available in cans in most Chinese stores.*

1 Put the flour, sugar and salt in a large mixing bowl and sprinkle in the yeast. Make a well in the centre and pour in the warm water. Mix to a dough. Place the dough on a floured board and knead for 10 minutes. Return it to the bowl, cover and set aside in a warm place to rise for 20 minutes or until it has doubled in bulk.

2 Knock back (punch down) the dough, knead it again, return it to the bowl and set aside in a warm place for 15 minutes. Roll out the dough on a floured board and shape it into a 30cm/12in long roll about 5cm/2in in diameter. Cut the roll into 2.5cm/1in slices and flatten each of these with a rolling pin to a thin round, about 10cm/4in across.

3 Holding a pastry round on the palm of one hand, spoon a tablespoon of the filling into the centre. Cup your hand so that the dough enfolds the filling, pleating and pinching it where necessary. Pinch off the excess dough at the top and seal with a twisting action. Sealing is important or the buns will gape when steamed. Fill the remaining dumplings in the same way.

4 Cut 5cm/2in squares of baking parchment. Stand a dumpling on each piece of paper in a steamer. Steam for 15 minutes. Serve immediately.

Suppliers

UNITED STATES

The House of Rice Store
3221 North Hayden Road
Scottsdale, AZ 85251
Tel: (480) 947 6698`

99 Ranch Market
140 West Valley Boulevard
San Gabriel CA 91776
Tel: (626) 307 8899

Hong Kong Supermarket
18414 Colima Road,
Los Angeles CA 91748
Tel: (626) 964 1688

Seafood City Supermarket
1340, 3rd Avenue, Chula Vista
San Jose, CA 91911
Tel: (619) 422 7600

Ai Hoa
860 North Hill Street
Los Angeles, CA 90026
Tel: (213) 482 4824`

Oriental Grocery
11827 Del Amo Boulevard
Cerritos, CA 90701
Tel: (310) 924 1029

Unimart American and
 Asian Groceries
1201 Howard Street
San Francisco, CA 94103
Tel: (415) 431 0326

Georgia Asian Foods, Etc.
1375 Prince Avenue
Atlanta, GA 30341
Tel: (404) 543 8624

Augusta Market Oriental Foods
2117 Martin Luther King
 Jr. Boulevard
Atlanta, GA 30901
Tel: (706) 722 4988

Hong Tan Oriental Food
2802 Capitol Street,
Savannah, GA 31404
Tel: (404) 233 6698

Khanh Tan Oriental Market
4051 Buford Highway NE
Atlanta, GA 30345
Tel: (404) 728 0393

Norcross Oriental Market
6062 Norcross-Tucker Road
Chamblee, GA 30341
Tel: (770) 496 1656

The Oriental Pantry
423 Great Road
Acton, MA 01720
Tel: (978) 264 4576

May's American Oriental
 Market
422 West University Avenue
Saint Paul, MN 55103
Tel: (651) 293 1118

Nevada Asian Market
2513 Stewart Avenue
Las Vegas, NV 89101
Tel: (702) 387 3373

Dynasty Supermarket
68 Elizabeth Street
New York, NY 10013
Tel: (212) 966 4943

Asian Supermarket
109 E. Broadway
New York, NY 10002
Tel: (212) 227 3388

Kam Man Food
 Products
200 Canal Street
New York, NY 10013
Tel: (212) 571 0330

Hang Hing Lee Grocery
33 Catherine Street
New York, NY 10013
Tel: (212) 732 0387

Oriental Market
670 Central Park Avenue
Yonkers, NY 10013
Tel: (212) 349 1979

Asian Foods Ltd
260–280 West Leigh Avenue
Philadelphia, PA 19133
Tel: (215) 291 9500

Golden Foods
 Supermarket
9896 Bellaire Road
Houston, TX 77036
Tel: (713) 772 7882

Welcome Food Centre
9810 Bellaire Boulevard
Houston, TX 77030
Tel: (718) 270 7789

UNITED KINGDOM

Wing Yip
375 Nechells Park Road, Nechells
Birmingham, B7 5NT
Tel: 0121 327 3838

Sing Fat Chinese Supermarket
334 Bradford Street, Digbeth
Birmingham, B5 6ES
Tel: 0121 622 5888

Makkah Oriental Food Store
148-150 Charminster Road
Bournemouth, BH8 8YY
Tel: 0120 277 7303

Ryelight Chinese Supermarket
48 Preston Street
Brighton, BN1 2HP
Tel: 0127 373 4954

Wai Yee Hong
Eastgate Oriental City
Eastgate Road, Eastville
Bristol, BS5 6XY
Tel: 0845 873 3388

Wing Yip
544 Purley Way,
Croydon, CR0 4NZ
Tel: 0208 688 4880

Hoo Hing Cash & Carry
Lockfield Avenue, Brimsdown
Enfield, EN3 7QE

Pat's Chung Ying Chinese
 Supermarket
199-201 Leith Walk
Edinburgh, EH6 8NX
Tel: 0131 554 0358

See Woo
Unit 5, The Point, 29, Saracen Street
Glasgow, G22 5H7
Tel: 0845 0788 818

Chung Ying Supermarket
254, Dobbies Loan
Glasgow, G4 OHS
Tel: 0141 333 0333

Rum Wong Supermarket
London Road
Guildford, GU1 2AF
Tel: 0148 345 1568

Seasoned Pioneers Ltd
101 Summers Road
Brunswick Business Park
Liverpool, L3 4BJ
Tel: 0151 709 9330

Loon Fung Supermarket
42–44 Gerrard Street
London, W1V 7LP
Tel: 0207 373 8305

New Loon Moon
 Supermarket
9a Gerrard Street
London, W1D 5PP
Tel: 0207 734 3887

Golden Gate Grocers
100–102 Shaftesbury Avenue
London, W1D 5EE
Tel: 0207 437 0014

New China Gate
18 Newport Place
London, WC1H 7PR
Tel: 0207 237 8969

New Peking Supermarket
59 Westbourne Grove
London, W2 4UA
Tel: 0207 928 8770

Newport Supermarket
28–29 Newport Court
London, WC2H 7PO
Tel: 0207 437 2386

See Woo Hong
18–20 Lisle Street
London, WC2H 7BA
Tel: 0207 439 8325

Wing Yip
395 Edgware Road
London, NW2 6LN
Tel: 0207 450 0422

Wing Yip
Oldham Road, Ancoats
Manchester, M4 5HU
Tel: 0161 832 3215

Woo Sang Supermarket
19–21 George Street, Chinatown
Manchester, M1 4HE
Tel: 0161 236 4353

Miah, A. and Co
20 Magdalen Street
Norwich, NR3 1HE
Tel: 0160 361 5395

Hoo Hing Commercial Centre
Freshwater Road
Chadwell Heath
Romford, RM8 1RX
Tel: 020 8548 3636
Website: www.hoohing.com

Wah-Yu Chinese Supermarket
145 High St
Swansea, SA1 1NE
Tel: 0179 265 0888

Hong Cheong
115 Oxford St
Swansea, SA1 3JJ
Tel: 0179 246 8411

Fox's Spices (mail order)
Mason's Road
Stratford-upon-Avon, CV37 9NF
Tel: 0178 926 6420

AUSTRALIA
Duc Hung Long Asian Store
95 The Crescent
Fairfield, NSW 2165
Tel: (02) 9728 1092

Foodtown Thai Kee Supermarket
393–399 Sussex Street
Sydney, NSW
Tel: (02) 9281 2202

Harris Farm Markets
Sydney Markets
Flemongton, NSW 2140
Tel: (02) 9746 2055

Asian Supermarkets Pty Ltd
116 Charters Towers Road
Townsville, QLD 4810
Tel: (07) 4772 3997

Burlington Supermarkets
Chinatown Mall
Fortitude Valley, QLD 4006
Tel: (07) 3216 1828

The Spice and Herb Asian Shop
200 Old Cleveland Road
Capalaba, QLD 4157
Tel: (07) 3245 5300

Western Australia Kongs
 Trading Pty Ltd
8 Kingscote Street
Kewdale, WA 6105
Tel: (08) 9353 3380

NEW ZEALAND
Golden Gate Supermarket &
 Wholesalers Ltd.
8–12 Teed Street, Newmarket
Auckland Tel: (09) 523 3373

Happy Super Market
660 Dominion Road,
Mt Roskill,
Auckland Tel: (09) 623 8220

Lim Garden Supermarket Centre
3 Edsel Street, Henderson,
Auckland Tel: (09) 835 2599

CANADA
Arirang Oriental Food Store
1324 10 Ave Sw # 30
Calgary, AB, T3C 0J2
Tel: (403) 228 0980

T & T Supermarket
222 Cherry Street
Toronto, ON, M5A 3L2
Tel: (416) 463 8113
Website: www.tnt-supermarket.com
(16 stores across the country)

Marché Hawai
1999 Marcel Laurin, Sain-Laurent
Montreal, QC
Tel: (514) 856 0226

Hing Shing Market
1757 Kingsway, Vancouver, BC
Tel: (604) 873 4938

Star Asian Food Centre
2053 41st Avenue
W Vancouver, BC
Tel: (604) 263 2892

Tin Cheung Market
6414 Victoria Drive
Vancouver, BC
Tel: (604) 322 9237

Western Oriental Market
101–1050 Kingsway
Vancouver, BC
Tel: (604) 876 4711

Wing Sang Meat & Vegetable Market
3755 Main Street
Vancouver, BC
Tel: (604) 879 6866

Index

Author's acknowledgements
I would like to thank Anness
Publishing for giving me the
privilege of writing the series on
regional Chinese cooking, a project
that is close to my heart. Most of
all I would like to thank my son
Christopher for his unstinting help
in the exhaustive testing and
refining of all the recipes. As a
chef and food writer in his own
right, his knowledge and attention
to detail have been of enormous
help. I would also like to thank all
my Chinese friends from Hubei,
Guangzhou and Beijing; and my
siblings and in-laws who
collectively represent Cantonese,
Shantou, Fujian and Hakka
cultures for enhancing my
knowledge and collection of
regional Chinese recipes. Last but
not least, my grateful thanks to
Lucy Doncaster for her infinite
patience in fine-tuning my text.

Publishers' acknowledgements
The publishers would also like to
thank the following for permission
to reproduce their images: p7tl
Redlink/Corbis; p7tr So Hing-Keung/
Corbis; p8 Chris Hellier/Corbis;
p9tl Iain Lasterton/Alamy;
p10bl Ron Yue/Alamy; p10br
Beaconstox/Alamy; p13t Jon
Arnold Images Ltd/Alamy; p13b
Ron Yue/Alamy; p14bl Henry
Westheim Photography/Alamy;
p21b Donall O Cleirigh/iStockphoto.
All other photographs © Anness
Publishing Ltd.